THE LISTENING ADVANTAGE

This outcome-based text offers principles and skill-building experiences for the critical competence of listening. It serves as an adaptable supplement for courses in communication and professional studies.

It draws from the author's HURIER Listening Model, which identifies six interrelated components of listening—hearing, understanding, remembering, interpreting, evaluating, and responding—and considers the skills required to achieve the specific outcomes related to each. Varied classroom activities, including discussion questions, group processes, and other instructional strategies, facilitate skill-building and the achievement of each Listening Outcome. The final section of the text identifies those outcomes that are particularly relevant to specific career applications and provides cases to facilitate discussion and illustrate listening challenges in each field. The outcome-based, modular format allows instructors maximum flexibility in adapting instructional materials to meet the needs of specific courses and time frames.

The Listening Advantage is an invaluable supplement for courses in communication studies and professional fields including education, healthcare, helping professions, law, management, and service.

Judi Brownell is a Professor at Cornell's School of Hotel Administration, SC Johnson College of Business. She teaches courses in organizational behavior, human resources, and management communication. She has extensive international teaching experience and her online eCornell executive courses are taken worldwide.

THE LISTENING ADVANTAGE

Outcomes and Applications

Judi Brownell

Routledge
Taylor & Francis Group

NEW YORK AND LONDON

First published 2020
by Routledge
52 Vanderbilt Avenue, New York, NY 10017

and by Routledge
2 Park Square, Milton Park, Abingdon, Oxon, OX14 4RN

Routledge is an imprint of the Taylor & Francis Group, an informa business

Library of Congress Cataloging-in-Publication Data
Names: Brownell, Judi, 1949- author.
Title: The listening advantage : outcomes and applications /
Judi Brownell.
Description: 1 [edition]. | New York : Routledge, 2019.
Identifiers: LCCN 2019016493| ISBN 9780815360520
(hardback) | ISBN 9780815360544 (pbk.)
Subjects: LCSH: Listening.
Classification: LCC BF323.L5 B662 2019 | DDC 153.6/8–dc23
LC record available at https://lccn.loc.gov/2019016493

ISBN: 978-0-8153-6052-0 (hbk)
ISBN: 978-0-8153-6054-4 (pbk)
ISBN: 978-1-351-11802-6 (ebk)

Typeset in Bembo
by Swales & Willis, Exeter, Devon, UK

To my husband, Gary

CONTENTS

PREFACE

If you teach courses in a communication program or in a field that prepares students for a professional career, it is likely that you already recognize the value of effective listening to your students' future success. Listening effectiveness helps students navigate the complexities and responsibilities of their personal, social, and professional lives. It positions them to be critical and informed consumers and contributing members of families, organizations, and communities. This is particularly important as individuals have to choose among competing messages (often including those on social media) and navigate through challenges posed by competitors, clients, supervisors, guests, older adults, and other groups with whom they regularly interact. Yet, the majority of textbooks—even those in the field of communication—devote relatively little time to this critical competency. Whether students expect to go into counseling, healthcare, teaching, law, management, or other professions, an understanding of the listening process and the ability to listen well offers a distinct advantage.

The Listening Advantage: Outcomes and Applications is outcome-based and provides a flexible and focused supplement to your primary textbook. The desired Listening Outcomes central to your students' specific interests and needs are identified so that instruction can readily be adapted to focus on those goals. While your course emphasizes the principles and concepts of your discipline, *The Listening Advantage* helps students identify personal goals and develop the listening skills they need for your specific application or context. Identifying and selecting the Listening Outcomes most relevant to your field—whether a general communication offering or a focused professional offering—enables you to adapt the material to different time frames and instructional goals.

This supplement takes a listening-centered approach to communication. Students are introduced to listening as a personal competence, a career necessity, and as a social responsibility. The personal and professional benefits of effective listening are emphasized in the context of an applied, outcome-based approach. A comprehensive framework for developing listening effectiveness, the HURIER Listening Model, is presented. This behavioral model suggests that listening can viewed as a process composed of six interrelated components: hearing, understanding, remembering, interpreting, evaluating, and responding. A set of four or more Listening Outcomes, or desired behavioral goals, is then provided for each of the six components of the HURIER model. Specific skills are described as they contribute to achieving each outcome, and can be developed through individual and group activities.

Students' efforts are focused by selecting the several outcomes associated with listening effectiveness in their field. Students seeking to work in healthcare require a different configuration of outcomes to be successful than do students who want to become lawyers. The final section of the text, "Applications," identifies those outcomes that are particularly relevant to various career applications—healthcare, education, business, etc.—and presents additional cases to help prepare students for the specific listening challenges they are likely to confront. If you instruct a communication offering, you may choose to take advantage of most or all of the material in Chapters 3–8, selecting outcomes and skill-building activities that will prepare your students to become effective listeners and communicators in multiple and varied listening situations (Table 0.1).

TABLE 0.1 Preface

Listening Components, Outcomes, Skills, and Activities		
Relationships	*Questions to Ask Yourself*	*Application Example: Healthcare*
Components of the HURIER Listening Model: hearing, understanding, remembering, interpreting, evaluating, responding	Are some listening *components* more important to your application than others? The HURIER Listening Model conceptualizes listening as a process involving six interrelated components. The importance of each component to listening effectiveness depends on the individual's purpose and the listening context or application	Component: hearing messages

(*Continued*)

TABLE 0.1 (Cont.)

<table>
<tr><td colspan="3">Listening Components, Outcomes, Skills, and Activities</td></tr>
<tr><td>Relationships</td><td>Questions to Ask Yourself</td><td>Application
Example: Healthcare</td></tr>
<tr>
<td>Listening Outcomes associated with each component</td>
<td>Given your listening application and its challenges, what specific outcomes are important to achieve? There are a number of specific outcomes associated with each component of the HURIER model. Evaluating messages is important to both a healthcare professional and a lawyer, but the specific outcome priorities may be different</td>
<td>Outcome H2: don't get distracted</td>
</tr>
<tr>
<td>Skills required to achieve each desired Listening Outcome</td>
<td>What skills are needed to achieve the desired outcome? Outcomes are behavioral; they can be achieved through the development of specific skills acquired in your classroom</td>
<td>Skill 1: reduce or eliminate external distractions</td>
</tr>
<tr>
<td>Activities develop and improve specific listening skills</td>
<td>What activities will help learners develop important skills? Once desired outcomes are identified, students participate in a variety of activities to develop essential listening skills</td>
<td>See list of activities associated with H2</td>
</tr>
<tr>
<td>Applications refer to the specific context or career where listening takes place</td>
<td>The importance of achieving each outcome may vary according to the application of concern</td>
<td></td>
</tr>
</table>

A table is provided in the "Applications" section that illustrates how desired Listening Outcomes are associated with each of the careers. This provides a guide to selecting the specific outcomes (goals) you would like your students to achieve as well as adapting text content and activities to the amount of class time you have available for listening instruction. You have the option of covering listening in one class session or ten, in a day or a month—whatever works in your teaching schedule. Given the modular nature of the text, students can also use it independently to develop selected listening competencies.

ACKNOWLEDGMENTS

It's the random acts of kindness, the support that often comes unexpectedly, that keeps me energized and focused on my writing. So many times I "get a little help" from my friends and colleagues, and that makes all the difference. It could be a word of encouragement, a cup of coffee, a thoughtful note, an offer to take on a task. I am surrounded by a community of wonderful people—and I'd like to thank every one of them. Some have been life-long friends and others, like the students who challenge and inspire me, have moved in and out of my window more quickly. Always, I can depend on my family to provide the balance and the encouragement that allows me to write; my sons Conor and Cody, who keep me grounded, their wives, who keep me energized, and the grandchildren, who make me laugh. I owe untold thanks to my husband Gary, who is always there for me, and who has been for as long as I can remember.

There are, too, special people who played a direct role in making this text possible. My sincere thanks go to Nicole Salazar and Brian Eschrich at Routledge, as well as all those involved in the production process, including Aneneosa Okocha, Laura Janusik, Haley Kranstuber Horstman, Tamsin Ballard and Dan Shutt.

PART I
The Listening Advantage

1

PERSONAL, SOCIAL, AND PROFESSIONAL BENEFITS TO LISTENING

Listening as a Personal Advantage

Listening is one of the most important skills you can develop. The question is, do you believe it? What would it take to convince you that building listening competence will have a powerful and lasting positive impact in helping you achieve both personal and professional goals? The purpose of this text is to make the benefits of listening so clear that you'll not only work to improve your skills in this class, but you will make continuous improvement a lifelong pursuit. The fact is that whether you are preparing for the first day of class or for the first day of a new job, your listening effectiveness will define your success. Think of it this way: you owe it to yourself to listen, to take advantage of all the opportunities that surround you, both in your career and in your daily personal activities. Your attitude will also influence your success; the LAW of Listening emphasizes that improving your *listening* behavior (L) requires both *ability* (A) and your *willingness* (W) to work hard at it!

Personal Listening Outcomes that Matter

Increase Your Popularity

Most people automatically gravitate toward someone who listens to them. Try this experiment. Next time you are in a social gathering, forget about talking. Just listen actively. Ask the person questions, nod your head to indicate your understanding, maintain strong eye contact. You'll discover that when you are engaged and demonstrate interest, you're the one that your friends and acquaintances want to talk with. Everyone wants to be heard, and when you listen you show that you care about the person speaking and value his or her ideas. When you also remember what you hear, you have the basis for continued conversation and a strengthened relationship.

Present Yourself Professionally

What does it mean to be "professional"? You hear the term a lot. People who are professional take their field of study, or job, or the task at hand seriously and try to do their very best at it. They are respected and respectful; they are viewed as confident, credible, and well-prepared. Other people not only pay attention to what they have to say, they also share information with them because they feel comfortable and valued.

For example, is there an interview in your future? If so, your ability to create a professional image through listening will give you a decided advantage over those who see an interview as just an opportunity to talk about themselves. When you demonstrate effective listening, the interviewer will think of you as someone who is engaging and self-confident.

Facilitate Learning

You can't learn unless you listen. Some people listen, but they do so selectively, only paying attention to the ideas they agree with or the topics they find easy and interesting. It's not unusual to find yourself struggling to stay focused on classes that you find "boring," or people who are talking about things you think are silly or difficult. You can readily see how expanding the variety of topics you listen to, and listening with the goal of learning in mind, can increase your knowledge and make you a more interesting communication partner. Of course, it can also improve your grades and your understanding of the world!

Listen to Social Media and the Internet

Statistics on the use of social media—to learn, to connect with friends, to engage with the world—make it clear that young people today depend heavily on this medium. Learning the skills of listening will help you to filter the thousands of messages that fill the internet and your inbox and respond to them appropriately. Assessing their importance, their credibility, and their relevance will help you to become a better consumer and decision-maker. Social media is pervasive, and learning more about how to benefit from the opportunities technology provides will give you a strong communication advantage.

Increase Mindfulness

Mindfulness is defined as the ability to be fully present "in the moment," aware of yourself and your surroundings. Often, it is easy to become overwhelmed by the responsibilities you face on a daily basis. Mindfulness suggests that you focus inward, becoming more aware of your sensations and insights as they are experienced. Listening facilitates this process by helping you reconnect with your thoughts and emotions. There are both physical and mental health benefits to mindfulness. To enjoy the full value of this activity it is important to practice on a regular basis, which involves finding a time and place to leave your frustrations and stressors behind and focus on the present.

The more conscious you are of the sounds that surround you, the more likely it is that you will come to enjoy "just listening" and increase your awareness of and pleasure in your aural surroundings. It may be the sounds you hear by the lake or in the woods; it may be at a concert or a ball game—wherever you are, sounds surround you. Wherever you are, your experience can be enriched by focusing on the listening experience.

Listening as a Social Responsibility

The *listening advantage* extends well beyond the ways in which you benefit personally from increasing your listening effectiveness. In addition to the personal benefits you derive, effective listening also directly impacts—and shapes—the world around you. In that regard, you can think of listening as a social responsibility, a competence you develop in order to ensure that when you go out into the larger society you behave in a manner that is fair, respectful, and engaged. Listening is part of the cultural context—it creates what is called the listening environment. Below we discuss a few personal listening advantages as well as the ways in which a commitment to effective listening can transform families, communities, and cultures into happier and healthier places to live and work.

Social Listening Outcomes that Matter

Make Responsible Decisions

The world is getting increasingly complex. The internet is accessible 24/7 and, as you know, messages come from all kinds of sources and in all forms and formats. There is virtually no location that is out of reach as technology transforms communication and alters the information we send and receive, dramatically changing what it means to listen.

As a member of this new social environment, you have a greater responsibility and challenge to make judgments about the accuracy and fairness of the information you receive. Only by preparing yourself to listen critically can you navigate this sea of often overwhelming information. Increasingly, your decisions affect others in often unanticipated ways—whether the issue is gun control, environmental protection, or choosing a site for an upcoming event.

Respect Individual Differences

As technology increases your ability to reach out, it becomes increasingly important to recognize that the people with whom you are interacting my not share your values, attitudes, or experiences. While you may find the person sitting next to you in class has different views on the topics covered in Government or Management, you'll discover—if you haven't already—that individual differences can be much more profound than simply point of view. The US population is aging, travel is becoming more frequent and there is a growing awareness of gender issues and how they impact communication effectiveness. Living in an increasingly diverse environment, and performing in a culturally diverse workplace, requires that you listen to understand and respect a range of beliefs, abilities, and value orientations.

Use Communication Media Responsibly

The nature and contexts of listening are rapidly changing as the world becomes forever connected in new and increasingly complex ways. Social media applications, in particular, have the potential to bring about significant consequences for large numbers of people, potentially on a global scale. There are few other contexts where listening is as critical to ensuring the well-being not only of individuals, but of organizations, communities, and countries. Young people, in particular, are well-positioned to have a profound impact on the world through the choices they make as they use the media to accomplish goals and explore new frontiers.

Recognize and Address Ethical Issues

At what point does something become your responsibility just because you know about it—just because you have listened? As a listener you will be confronted with a range of decisions and dilemmas. Some will be simple, straightforward, and easily resolved. Others, not so much. While you may think you behave ethically and have a clear compass to guide your personal behavior, what happens when you are confronted with decisions that have a clear benefit, but may cross the line in terms of their ethical implications? What do you do when you become aware of classmates or colleagues who are behaving in ways you believe bring harm to others? As you become a more critical and informed listener you will undoubtedly face difficult dilemmas as you participate in teams, organizations, and the larger social environment. What will you do?

2

AN OUTCOMES APPROACH TO LISTENING

Introduction

While we've established that there are a lot of good reasons to listen, this text focuses on the advantages of effective listening in the workplace and on the positive, important outcomes that will distinguish your performance. At first you might think, "Well, everyone listens..." Not true! You'll find, as you become more aware of listening behaviors, that this is far from the case. You'll discover that the "Listening Advantage" will provide you with a competitive advantage in all of your career activities, from blowing away the competition in an employment interview to learning your job requirements to quickly assessing those often unspoken aspects of the organization that determine your ultimate success. Then there's networking, professional development, and moving up the career ladder.

By working to become an excellent listener, you'll not only differentiate yourself; you'll also foster a healthier and more productive workplace. While excellent listeners perform their own jobs more effectively than do poor listeners, they also create a positive "listening environment." Fostering a strong listening culture results in positive outcomes for your entire team, department, or organization; your colleagues feel valued and respected and everyone benefits from being in an environment where people listen. There seems to be no question that listening facilitates compassion and caring in the workplace. Effective listeners more readily develop meaningful relationships with colleagues, increasing overall job satisfaction and commitment.

You're not likely to put a lot of effort into developing your listening skills unless you know there's some purpose, some benefit. That's why we've emphasized how important it is to listen well, and why we'll now show you how this essential skill can be developed and how you can achieve a variety of listening outcomes. While all listening behaviors are useful, we will present a model that allows you to focus on those most relevant to specific career-related responsibilities and contexts.

First, you'll need to learn about a simple approach to listening called the HURIER model. Its six components cover just about every listening situation you'll encounter. Each listening component in the model encompasses a number of listening "outcomes." Outcomes are the goals you want to achieve as an effective listener—the things you want to be able to do when you are in a communication situation. You accomplish each outcome by mastering a set of listening skills. A variety of experiential activities, discussion questions and group activities help you practice and develop these life-long skills.

Listening-Centered Communication

Our perspective in this text is called *listening-centered communication*. Rather than taking the traditional view of communication—where your first thought is, "What will I say?!" or "Wait until they hear this!"—we focus instead on your role as a listener, on the critical task of gathering as much information as you can to better understand the other person. The more you know about your communication partner(s), the better prepared you will be to create messages that will be effective and accomplish your purpose—to inform, persuade, entertain, inspire. Getting to know someone includes not only focusing on what they say, or who they text, or how they gesture, but also taking into consideration what they have previously experienced, what goals they seek, and what attitudes and values influence their thinking. The communication context—where you are, who else is there, the purpose for getting together—also becomes important as it shapes and defines the interactions that take place.

The second distinguishing characteristic of our approach to communication is that it is relational—the functions of speaking and listening really can't be separated completely. Effective communicators are listening as they speak in order to assess the effectiveness of their messages. They look for clues—whether it be nonverbal cues or number of hits—about interest, understanding, emotional responses—and adapt accordingly. In some contexts, their response to feedback from their listeners is immediate. In other cases, such as texting and other online communication, messages are modified over time. This means, of course, that in the role of "listener" you are also responding in ways that let your partner know whether her message has been effective—and whether or not you have listened. You can see why it's often difficult or impossible to distinguish, at any particular point, the speaker from the listener.

Applications of the HURIER Listening Model

Let's say you want to go into the field of law. You're really good at listening to arguments, determining whether the evidence presented is sufficient and whether you can make a good case to support your position on the issue. When it comes to developing close relationships, however, your record is pretty bleak. You've been told repeatedly that you "don't listen," and you have to admit that as soon as someone begins telling you about their weekend adventures and what they like for breakfast, your thoughts immediately wander. Listening to a long presentation requires a very different set of skills than listening to a child explain her craft project. This fact is nowhere more apparent than in the workplace, where each different career and role necessitates a specific, and often distinctive, set of listening behaviors to achieve the listening outcomes that will increase your effectiveness.

Since our focus is on preparing you to listen with confidence in your career, the important thing is to make sure that your personal listening strengths align with the competencies you will need to be effective in your professional activities. This doesn't happen automatically. It requires that you:

1. determine which specific listening outcomes are required for your career success
2. identify the skills that will help you achieve your goals
3. create SMART goals and an action plan for developing those behaviors that will have the most impact on your performance (see Chapter 9)

The HURIER Listening Model (Figure 2.1) was developed in response to the need for better definition and development of the listening behaviors that matter. Researchers realized that when employees say, "She doesn't listen," different people mean very different things. Some mean that their doctor doesn't focus on their specific concerns even though they emphasize them in conversation. Others are responding to the fact that while their manager always agrees to take a particular action, he seldom follows up on his promises. Still others are frustrated because even when discussing important safety concerns, their sales representative seems distracted and indifferent.

The HURIER model of listening, then, addresses six distinctive but interrelated components of the listening process—hearing, understanding, remembering, interpreting, evaluating, and responding (Box 2.1). *Hearing* draws attention to your focus and concentration—were you paying attention to what was said? Or were you disinterested and distracted? *Understanding* is also a skill that can be improved through a variety of techniques as you come to realize that sharing meanings is not nearly as easy as it might seem. The "R" stands for *remembering*. Other people will assume that you didn't listen if you don't keep your promises or remember what they told you. Nonverbal

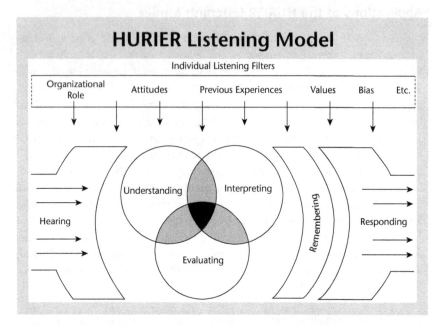

FIGURE 2.1 HURIER Listening Model

communication also plays a key role in shaping perceptions of listening effectiveness. Attending to nonverbal cues improves your ability to accurately *interpret* what the speaker means. You consider her feelings and emotional response as well as her words. *Evaluating* is just that—analyzing the message and taking a position on the topic. By recognizing how quickly you make judgments, and how often people draw conclusions without considering sufficient evidence, you can improve your critical listening skills with just a little practice. Finally, your partner, your team, your audience, or "friends" you have met online, judge the quality of your listening by your *response*. Becoming more aware of this behavior is part of being a skilled listener and an effective communicator. Each cluster, with accompanying outcomes, will be more or less important to you depending on your career focus and future needs. This text will help you determine where to put your energy in achieving those listening outcomes that will make the most difference to you in accomplishing your professional responsibilities.

Listening Outcomes and Contexts

Your goal is to distinguish yourself as someone who listens. You can earn respect and credibility by demonstrating skills in one or more of the six components of the HURIER model. To facilitate your learning, each of the following chapters (Chapters 3–8) addresses one listening component and its set

BOX 2.1 COMPONENTS OF THE HURIER LISTENING MODEL

Hearing

In order to hear, you first need to pay attention! Knowing what to focus on is the first step in becoming an effective listener. Often, hearing well takes planning—you may need to position yourself where you can hear, or take other actions so that your ability to listen isn't derailed by internal or external distractions. Listening is especially difficult in diverse environments, whether those differences are cultural, age-related, or simply a matter that your interests aren't shared with the speaker.

Understanding

Understanding, what we call listening comprehension, is often taken for granted. Creating shared meanings—ensuring that the message we receive is what the speaker intended—is a complex process. Interruptions are one of the most common barriers because they prevent the speaker from fully expressing her thought. Listeners are often quick to make assumptions; unless they check their perceptions, they may not even realize that what they think they heard is not what the speaker meant!

Remembering

Remembering is essential in order for listeners to apply the information they receive. There's a better chance of remembering something if you use both your visual and your auditory senses. Using one of many memory strategies, most likely those that include visual imagery techniques, can greatly improve your ability to recall what you heard. While personal variables influence your memory, stress is particularly significant because it prevents you from concentrating on what the other person is saying.

Interpreting

When you interpret messages, you go beyond the speaker's words and take into account the total communication situation, which includes the emotional message conveyed by the speaker's nonverbal behaviors. Voice, body posture, facial expression, eye contact—all are part of the message. Empathic listeners not only focus on the speaker's nonverbal cues, they also let their partner know through their own verbal and nonverbal behavior that they understand. Each person's background and past experiences dramatically influence his or her interpretations and reactions.

Evaluating

When you're bombarded with messages it's particularly important to have some way of distinguishing valid and reliable information from propaganda and emotional appeals. When you evaluate what you hear, you ask yourself questions that will enable you to determine whether what someone says is a fact or an assumption, whether they are biased or objective, and whether the evidence they present is sufficient to support their point. It is also important to view incoming information with an ethical lens to ensure that decisions and behavior bring no harm to others.

Responding

Effective communicators recognize the range of responses available to them. Developing behavioral flexibility is key to listening effectiveness; in any given situation, you might present facts, offer support, ask a question, show compassion, or answer in any number of other ways. Two response styles that are of particular value are a) assertive responses, and b) supportive responses. In each case, you are likely to have not only accomplished your purpose but also improved your relationship.

of associated behavioral outcomes. Your goal, then, is to identify the outcomes of most importance to you, and then to achieve them by mastering the accompanying set of listening skills. You develop these relevant skills through a variety of individual and group activities.

While all six components of the HURIER Listening Model are important, the context in which you're communicating influences which skills are most essential for effectiveness. It makes a difference whether you are in a restaurant, at a meeting, or on a sports team. Your listening requirements change from one situation to the next; listening on your cell phone is a different experience than listening to instructions for your final exam.

It would be great if you could spend all the time you wanted to develop amazing listening skills. Since that's probably not the case, this book individualizes your instruction by suggesting where you can best spend your time to be effective in the situations that are most important to you. In the "Applications" section, you can select the career most closely aligned with your course or with your future aspirations, and give more focused attention to developing the skills required in that particular listening context.

Sometimes it is helpful to clearly define a personal goal and then make a concrete action plan to achieve it. One effective goal-setting method, called the SMART process, is suggested in Box 2.2. SMART goals, explained in

---

BOX 2.2 CREATE SMART GOALS

Goal-setting is prerequisite to achieving your listening outcomes. By creating a SMART goal for each skill you want to master, you will be able to accurately assess improvement in your listening ability.

S: Specific Goals are focused on *concrete behaviors*, stated as something you can observe.

M: Measurable You can determine how close you are to meeting your goal by specifying *how* you will measure achievement.

A: Attainable Goals are realistic—you can achieve them within a reasonable period of time.

R: Relevant Goals are central to your personal and career success.

T: Time-bound Goals have a completion deadline.

As you make choices about where to focus your energy, it's important to identify what we call "high-leverage activities." Those are the things that have the most value, not only now but in the future. The ability to listen well is at the top of this list. You'll never regret spending your time learning to listen.

---

more detail in Chapter 9, are helpful because they describe your goals in a way that enables you to clarify your target behavior, set a deadline, and determine if your objectives have been met.

Recommended Reading for Part I

Bodie, G.D. (2017). Measuring the behavioral components of listening. In *The Sourcebook of Listening Research: Methodology and Measures*, pp. 123–150. D. Worthington & G.D. Bodie (eds). Hoboken, NJ: John Wiley and Sons.

Bostrom, R. N. (2011). Rethinking conceptual approaches to the study of listening. *International Journal of Listening*, 25, 10–26.

Boyatzis, R. E., Stubbs, E. C., & Taylor, S. N. (2002). Learning cognitive and emotional intelligence competencies through graduate management education. *Academy of Management Learning and Education*, 1(2), 150–162.

Brownell, J. (1994). Teaching listening: Some thoughts on the behavioral approach. *Business Communication Quarterly*, 57(4), 19–26.

Brownell, J. (2010). Listening leaders: The skills of listening-centered communication. In *Listening and Human Communication in the 21st Century*, pp. 141–157. A. Wolvin (ed.). West Sussex: Blackwell.

Brownell, J. (2018). *Listening: Attitudes, Principles, & Skills*, 6thedn. Routledge: Taylor & Francis.

Coetzer, M. F., Bussin, M., & Geldenhuys, M. (2017). The functions of a servant leader. *Administrative Sciences*, 7(1), 5–6.

Guy, N. (2018). Listening with influence. *Research World*, 72, 44–54.

Keaton, S. A. & Worthington, D. L. (2018). Listening in mediated contexts: Introduction to a special issue. *International Journal of Listening*, 32(2), 1–4.

Lazenby, N. & Lubinsky, D. (2018). Listen up or lose out. *Internal Auditing*, 33(5), 41–42.

Macnamara, J. (2017). Toward a theory and practice of organizational listening. *International Journal of Listening*, 32, 1–23.

Patterson, K. A. (2000). *Servant Leadership: A Theoretical Model*. Doctoral dissertation, Regent University, AAT3082719.

Purdy, M. (1997). What is listening? In *Listening in Everyday Life: A Personal and Professional Approach*, pp. 3–9. M. Purdy & D. Borisoff (eds). Lanham, MD: University Press of America.

Remedios, L., Clarke, D., & Hawthorne, L. (2008). Framing collaborative behaviors: Listening and speaking in problem-based learning. *Interdisciplinary Journal of Problem-Based Learning*, 2(1), 1–20.

Russell, R. F. & Stone, A. G. (2002). A review of servant leadership attributes: Developing a practical model. *Leadership & Organization Development* Journal, 23(4), 145–157.

Schramm, P. (2017). Listening to drive culture change. *Strategic HR Review*, 16(4), 161–165.

Shaughan, K. & Worthington, D. L. (2018). Listening in mediated contexts: Introduction to a special issue. *International Journal of Listening*, 32, 65–68.

Spataro, S. E. & Bloch, J. (2018). "Can you repeat that?" Teaching active listening in management education. *Journal of Management Education*, 42(2), 168–198.

Sterling, L. (2017). You're talking but is anyone listening? *Strategic HR Review*, 16(5), 211–215.

Washington, R. R., Sutton, C. D., & Field, H. S. (2006). Individual differences in servant leadership: The roles of values and personality. *Leadership & Organization Development Journal*, 27(8), 700–716.

Wolvin, A. & Brownell, J. (2008). Listening into the Future Chapter 3. In *Curriculum Development and Assessment*, pp. 101–135. J. N. Casey & R. E. Upton (eds). Hauppauge, NY: Nova Publishers.

Worthington, G.D. (2017). Modeling and measuring cognitive components of listening. In *The Sourcebook of Listening Research: Methodology and Measures*, pp. 70–96. D. Worthington & G. D. Bodie (eds). Hoboken, NJ: John Wiley and Sons.

PART II

Listening Outcomes and the Skills to Achieve Them

3

LISTEN TO HEAR

Outcomes

You'll only know what's going on if you focus your attention on the other person and concentrate on what he has to say. Knowing what is most important to listen to among all the various messages you hear is also essential. Often, hearing well takes planning—you may need to position yourself close to the speaker or turn down the air conditioning. Listening is especially difficult when you are communicating with someone whose first language isn't English, or if the speaker's voice is too soft to be easily heard. While most listening is purposeful, what we call appreciative listening takes place when you turn your focus to the sounds that you find peaceful, relaxing, and enjoyable.

Listening Outcome H1: Focus Attention on the Right Things

What? Never mind. Just pay attention. Far too many listening problems are the result of not hearing what the speaker said, and there are more reasons than you can imagine that explain when and how things go wrong. First, you can't hear unless you have focused your attention. The next time you leave an event with someone, find out what they recall. You're walking to the car with a friend following a presentation on travel in France. She begins talking excitedly about the fact that one of her favorite wines comes from a winery near your destination. You honestly didn't even pick up on the fact that you could tour wineries—in fact, you were feeling a little annoyed because she didn't seem to have paid any attention to what you consider the important points, such as transportation costs and the cheapest places to stay. What's most important? Well, it depends.

Skills for Success

1. Decide What's Most Important

Listening requires that you deliberately direct your attention to make sure you hear what you intend. Hearing—the kind of focused concentration you need to do when you listen—is not automatic. Sure, you hear loud noises—a siren in the background or a piece of glass dropped next to you. Generally, however, you are the master of what gets into your head (and, as we'll later discuss, what stays there!). You control your focus. Accepting the fact that you're not a victim—you are an active participant in the listening process who hears what you decide to hear—is the first step toward successful communication.

2. Plan Ahead So You Don't Miss What You Need to Hear

Whether you are engaged in a conversation with one person or six, whether you are listening to a lecture or a video, it helps a lot if you prepare yourself in advance. Bring questions with you, take notes, and keep in mind that it is your responsibility to hear the information that has the most value to you. You know you can't pay attention to everything, and you know how easy it is to get distracted by things that seem more interesting at the time. If you prepare to listen in advance, and follow through with your plan, you won't have regrets!

3. Expand Your Interests

There's no inherently dull subject, just listeners who haven't connected the subject to their personal interests and needs. If the speaker doesn't do this for you, then it's up to you to find good reasons to listen. Think about the ways the information may help you in the future, or if it would make a good story or help out someone else. Just as a positive attitude helps you overcome many life challenges, a positive mental attitude makes a significant difference in your listening effectiveness as well. If you see no need to listen, then you might as well spend your time doing something else! Remember the LAW of listening—L for listening; A for ability; W for willingness. It's not all about your skills. Motivation (W for willingness) is also key.

Activities to Focus Your Attention

Activity 1

Three individuals take positions in different corners of a room. Two additional people are designated as "listeners."

a) Each of the three individuals positioned around the room thinks of a recent trip they've taken or an experience they've enjoyed. Their goal is to gain the listeners' attention over the other two speakers by talking about their subject in an interesting and engaging manner (not by being loudest!).

When everyone is ready, the presentations begin simultaneously and continue for approximately two minutes.

b) After the time is up, each speaker asks the designated listeners a question about their presentation. Keep going around with questions from each of the three speakers until you can draw some conclusions about which presentations were heard and which didn't generate as much focus of attention.

c) Discuss the types of information and delivery that helped establish attention on a particular message.

Activity 2

a) Attend an event—perhaps a farmer's market, trade show, or sports event. Close your eyes and listen. What sounds or activities attract your attention? What types of sound stand out for you? Which fade into the background?

b) Do this exercise with a friend and compare what you heard. Why might there be differences in where you and your friend focus your attention?

Activity 3
What specific sounds attract your attention?

a) Make a list of sounds that you almost always hear, and those that you find easy to ignore. Try to determine the reasons for these differences.

b) List the sounds that help you concentrate and the ones that distract you. Where are you when you hear each type of sound? Are they the same for everyone?

Activity 4
Describe a common situation in which you find yourself, and where you always have difficulty paying attention.

a) Create a list of the specific actions you can take to prepare yourself to listen effectively in spite of the distractions around you.

b) The next time you are in this listening situation, try out some of the suggestions on your list. Which were most effective?

Activity 5
Sit in a circle with eight to ten of your classmates.

a) Collectively, select a topic from the following list.

- The most memorable adventures I've had with my family.
- Animals in the wild.

- Why pets are so much fun.
- How to be a super student.
- Space travel.

b) Choose a member of your group to begin talking on the chosen topic. After they have spoken for about two minutes, the person to the left takes over and continues speaking on the same topic. If someone hasn't had first-hand experience on the topic, they are welcome to make up stories. Repeat this until at least six individuals have had a turn.

- Who was easiest to listen to?
- Who did the best job of holding your attention?
- Describe the characteristics that made some people easier to focus on than others.
- What do the results of this exercise tell you about hearing?

Activity 6
Try the following exercise.

a) List five topics that you are interested in and five that you find "boring."
b) After recording each topic in the far-left column, rate the amount of expertise you feel you have on the subject.
c) Next, indicate how easy or difficult you find the particular subject to understand.

Fascinating	*Know a Little*					*Know a Lot*		*Difficult*		
Easy										
1. _____	5	4	3	2	1	5	4	3	2	1
2. _____	5	4	3	2	1	5	4	3	2	1
3. _____	5	4	3	2	1	5	4	3	2	1
4. _____	5	4	3	2	1	5	4	3	2	1
5. _____	5	4	3	2	1	5	4	3	2	1
Boring										
1. _____	5	4	3	2	1	5	4	3	2	1
2. _____	5	4	3	2	1	5	4	3	2	1
3. _____	5	4	3	2	1	5	4	3	2	1
4. _____	5	4	3	2	1	5	4	3	2	1
5. _____	5	4	3	2	1	5	4	3	2	1

Review the information you've gathered.

a)   What generalizations can you make from what you observed?
b)   Do the topics you enjoy seem to be easier or more difficult than the ones
     you find boring? What else might you conclude from your ratings?

Listening Outcome H2: Don't Get Distracted

You can't concentrate. Right now, as you're reading this text, stop for a
moment. What is distracting you? Distractions that affect your listening can be
either internal or external. That is, you can be distracted by your personal
thoughts and emotions as easily as by things in your external environment. An
upcoming exam, a recent message about a friend's illness, or just feeling
excited about an athletic event is enough to keep you from fully concentrating
on the key message.

Maybe you had to skip breakfast to make it to class and you're hungry. Or
maybe you stayed up too late finishing a paper and can't seem to keep your
eyes open. Fatigue is one of the most difficult internal distractions to overcome
and one of the most troublesome for listeners. Then there's the physical environment—where are you? External distractions often prevent listeners from
hearing messages, whether they are received face-to-face or through some
form of technology. Perhaps you get a phone call but your friend, who is
standing next to you, doesn't stop talking. Or you're sitting outside and a
huge truck goes by. Or perhaps you're in class and the sun is coming through
the window and you're too hot. Maybe the air conditioner is blowing right
on you and you're too cold.

The challenge of concentration affects everyone, but sometimes the
message is too important to miss and zoning out is not an option. Recall,
too, that it's much easier to concentrate on things that you already find
interesting. If you're a sports fan, hearing about how the teams placed
may be exciting to you, but how about for your partner? Not so much.
The key here is not to make assumptions and discount the value of a message before you even try to listen. Take charge of your mental energy and
focus!

Skills for Success

1. Reduce or Eliminate External Distractions
Begin by tuning in to all the potential distractions in your environment.
There's that ball game going on outside your window. Do you have to sit
where you know you'll be distracted? You're taking a class that wasn't your
first choice (or second, or third. . .) and you sit in the back where, no surprise,

you are tempted to do homework for another class or check your text messages. This behavior is not going to help with your listening effectiveness. Better to move up front where you have fewer possible distractions. Sit where the speaker can see you (most A-grade students are in the first three rows of the class!). Staying active, and being proactive, will also help to focus your thoughts on the task at hand. Take notes, ask questions; do whatever you can to engage with both the speaker and the material.

2. Reduce or Eliminate Internal Distractions
Internal distractions, believe it or not, are more difficult to control than those in your physical environment. Worry. Excitement. Anger. Fear. Certainly, whenever you are emotional about something, it is hard to get it out of your mind. Meditation or some other type of relaxation technique will sometimes help to get beyond the strong emotional response so you can begin to focus on the situation at hand.

Internal distractions also include things that are easier to identify and manage. Are you too hungry to sit and listen? Go eat something! Cold? Turn on the heat! Sometimes we think it's most appropriate to ignore internal discomforts but, in the end, they keep you from focusing on important information that you may not be able to recover.

3. Address Issues Created by the Thought-Speech Differential
One thing that makes it difficult to concentrate is the *thought-speech differential*. What that means is that you think—or process incoming information—really fast. In fact, if the speech was clear and you were familiar with the vocabulary, you could probably listen effectively to someone who speaks three times faster than normal. A lot of speakers talk slowly, and that makes it particularly difficult for you to listen well. The "differential" between your rate of information processing and the rate of speaking results in a lot of free mental processing time—time that allows you to daydream, check your text messages, think about what you'll have for lunch, or watch your baseball team practicing just outside the window.

What can you do? First, become aware of your "slack" time. There's no magic; you need to be willing to put in the effort required to focus your mental energy and stay on track. That means, instead of allowing yourself to indulge in fantasies and daydreams, you force yourself to mentally review what the speaker just said. This deliberate focus and review of the message is called the Vocalized Listening Technique (see Box 3.1), which is simply a form of "self-talk." Another way to improve your concentration is to pose questions to yourself regarding the purpose of the message, review the main points in your mind, and ask yourself further questions related to the topic.

BOX 3.1 THE VOCALIZED LISTENING TECHNIQUE, OR SELF-TALK

When it comes to listening, talking to yourself is a good thing! This inner speech can take many forms and has a number of applications for hearing, understanding, and remembering.

1   Repeat portions of the speaker's message to yourself silently. This will help you store them in your memory as well as keep your mind on the speaker.
2   Ask yourself questions about the ideas being presented. Make sure you not only hear, but understand, what was said.
3   Relate what you hear to your personal interests and needs—make connections and give yourself good reasons to listen.
4   Stay focused! Do whatever you can to actively engage in the communication process—sit close to the speaker, stay away from distractions, sit in an alert position.

Activities to Reduce Distractions

Activity 1
Reflect on your current behaviors.

a)   What internal distractions have you most recently experienced? What thoughts do you find particularly difficult to ignore?
b)   Can you associate your distractions with a particular emotion—happiness, fear, anxiety, anger?
c)   What do you currently do when emotions interfere with your ability to concentrate? What habits have you developed to compensate for any lack of concentration?

Activity 2
Identify three specific individuals you believe are excellent speakers. Then, with some of your classmates, discuss the characteristics these individuals display. Make a list of your findings.

a)   What do these speakers do to hold your attention?
b)   Would you say they speak generally faster or slower than average?
c)   What do they do to engage you in the communication?
d)   Do they do anything that distracts you from their message? If so, what is it?

Activity 3
Describe a recent situation where you were successful in overcoming external distractions.

a) What was the situation? What was distracting you?
b) What did you do to maintain your focus on the speaker and continue listening?

Activity 4
Not everyone is distracted by the same things. Choose a situation where you have to concentrate—perhaps listening to a lecture or doing your homework. Look at the following list and rate, on a scale of 1 (not distracting) to 10 (extremely distracting), how readily you would be distracted by each item.

Item	Not Distracting		Somewhat Distracting			Extremely Distracting	
1. Laughter near you	1	2	3	4	5	6	7
2. Someone playing a videogame	1	2	3	4	5	6	7
3. Music you enjoy	1	2	3	4	5	6	7
4. Heavy equipment	1	2	3	4	5	6	7
5. A crowd cheering at an event	1	2	3	4	5	6	7

Compare your ratings to those of your classmates. Are they similar? What could cause discrepancies among you and your friends?

Activity 5
Think about your daily listening experiences and make a list of situations where the Vocalized Listening Technique (Box 3.1) might be useful. If you regularly listen to presentations or speeches, that might be a good opportunity to practice. Choose two recurring situations, and set a goal of trying this technique at least twice. Did you notice any difference in your ability to focus? Discuss your experience with your classmates.

Activity 6
Get together with several of your classmates and create a list of well-known personalities. Select some who speak relatively slowly, and others who speak quickly. They might be entertainers, political figures, or anyone likely to be familiar to all members of your group. When you have three or more names in each list, discuss the effectiveness and "listenability" of each person. What factors contribute to your ability to focus on what they're saying? Explain.

Listening Outcome H3: Hear the Message Accurately

Poor hearing can affect both you and your listening partner. For some reason, most people hate to admit that they have a hearing problem. Hearing loss is a common result of aging, yet many older adults are reluctant to get their hearing tested or to wear devices that make it easier to hear.

You can imagine the communication problems that occur as a result of not hearing well. Rather than continuing to ask the speaker to repeat what was said, the listener begins to make assumptions. As the conversation continues, communication breaks down even further until subsequent misunderstandings create significant problems either for the relationship or for the task that needed to be accomplished. If you interact regularly with an older adult or someone who has hearing difficulties, you can probably think of numerous examples where the two of you were clearly not on the same page! Of course, hearing can also be an issue when a background sound is so loud that normal speech becomes nearly impossible to distinguish. Think night clubs, construction sites, concerts, or other public places where loud noise can either be pleasant, or not!

Finally, sometimes a person simply speaks so softly that you don't catch what she says (and no one else does, either!). It's not you, it's her—but your ability to listen and respond is still your responsibility, so regardless of the situation it is up to you to figure out a way to "get the message." No one feels comfortable continually saying, "Could you please speak up? I'm having trouble hearing you, please speak a little louder!" However, giving up and just pretending to listen doesn't help much either. Listening when technology is involved, over the phone, on conference calls, using Skype or Zoom, creates even more challenges to hearing.

Skills for Success

1. Be Proactive
Can't hear very well? The first thing is to ask yourself if you should move! If you can't hear where you are, would you be able to hear any better if you stood closer, or farther away, or shut a window to block out ambient noise? Whenever you find yourself thinking, "Poor me. It's too noisy and I can't hear," begin to explore your options—don't be a victim of your environment.

2. Have Your Hearing Checked
No one likes to think that they are losing their hearing. While hearing aids are likely to become fashion accessories like eye glasses, the moment has not yet arrived. That's no excuse. If you are having a problem hearing—if other people around you can hear things that you can't—it's time to have a hearing exam. There are many options and, even if you find that your hearing is fine, that piece of information is also good to know.

3. Maintain a Positive Listening Attitude
Effective listeners work to create good reasons to listen. They partner with the speaker to search for ways to link their interests and needs to the speaker's message. This takes work, but the mental focus of making this connection also improves your hearing. As soon as you tell yourself the message isn't important, that it doesn't really matter and you don't care whether or not you hear it, your listening is doomed!

In addition, you've probably heard of selective perception—our tendency to listen to those messages that confirm our already-held beliefs. If your goal is accurate hearing, you will only be successful if you expose yourself to positions and points of view that are foreign to you—and work at carefully listening to the entire message. In today's classrooms and workplaces you will undoubtedly encounter people whose life experiences, values, motives, and attitudes are different from your own. Hearing their messages accurately, and being open to and positive about their views, is critical to creating healthy listening environments. The power of a positive attitude can't be overestimated; your predispositions and preferences influence every message you hear.

Activities to Assist in Hearing the Message Accurately

Activity 1
Everyone thinks they have good hearing; of course, you don't really know if you're missing something because you can't hear it! Sit in a public area where there are a lot of different sounds, like the lobby of a student union, a mall, or a cafeteria. What do you hear?

a)   Make a list of the sounds that come to the forefront and those that fade.
b)   For each category, try to determine common characteristics that would account for your placement. Perhaps it's the pitch, or the distance from where you're sitting. Or you may hear male voices more clearly that female voices. Become more aware of what you hear and why some sounds resonate more than others. Remember, this isn't about the messages, it's just about the voices and the sounds around you.
c)   What conclusions can you draw from this activity?

Activity 2
Stand back-to-back with a partner and begin a conversation.

a)   As you speak, take a step forward—your partner will do the same. Keep up the conversation. Wait a minute or so and take another step.
b)   As soon as one of you can't hear well, shout out and stop the activity.
c)   Discuss all of the factors that contribute to effective hearing, both verbal and nonverbal. Was it strange to talk, back-to-back, at a distance? Why?

Activity 3
On many occasions, hearing is reduced because of speaker variables.

a) Create a list of the ways in which speakers make it difficult for you to hear what they say.
b) As a listener, what might you do to reduce the impact of these behaviors or characteristics on the communication situation?
c) Think of your own communications. Do people ever complain about not being able to hear you? What do they say about your voice?

Activity 4
Consider how your attitude influences your listening.

a) Identify a recent occasion where you found yourself disagreeing strongly with what the speaker was saying.
b) How was your listening affected? Did you hear everything the speaker said? Were your "take-aways" accurate—were they what the speaker intended?
c) What can you do when you find yourself listening (maybe even in a class!) to a speaker you don't think is credible or who you don't think understands you or your situation? How can you ensure that you give the communicator a chance to be accurately heard?

Activity 5
It's important to recognize how technology affects your concentration. Texting, cell calls, other technology-based communications are often fleeting but may interrupt a conversation or make a friend feel like what she has to say is unimportant.

a) What impact do you feel texting and cell phones have on concentration in the three contexts below?

   a) meals with your family
   b) conversations with friends
   c) concentrating in classes

b) In a small group, create guidelines for the use of cell phones in your classes. You are welcome to recommend that they be used without reservation if you don't believe they affect the focus of your attention or the quality of your listening!

Activity 6
When you communicate through some type of mediated communication—cell phones, Zoom, video conferencing, and other technologies—hearing difficulties are even more likely to arise.

a)   Research this issue and determine what hearing problems are common to mediated communication.
b)   As communication through these channels becomes more common place, what can be done to ensure that accurate hearing is facilitated?

Listening Outcome H4: Engage in Appreciative Listening

While there's really no such thing as "just listening," you may find that what we call appreciative listening helps you reduce the stress of your studies or your workplace. Most of the listening you do takes a lot of energy. In fact, listening effectively is more difficult and requires more mental focus than speaking! Appreciative listening is simply letting go and allowing yourself to enjoy the sounds around you, whether that means a walk through the woods or a concert in the park.

Skills for Success

1. Heighten Your Awareness of Your Surroundings
Heightening your awareness of the sounds in your environment will almost automatically increase your appreciation of the ways in which listening impacts your daily experiences. Appreciative listening may be easy, but it doesn't just happen. You need to make time in your day to explore the sounds that surround you and the ways in which listening can help you relax and enjoy simple pleasures. How often do you currently stop and "just listen"? Probably not often enough!

2. Focus On the Journey
As you practice appreciative listening, you are likely to identify new listening experiences and opportunities. Often your focus is on the destination, the "mission," rather than the journey. While appreciative listening might be an end in itself, it also compliments other activities and enriches your experience regardless of your end goal. Once you begin to make appreciative listening a habit, you will likely be surprised at all the enjoyment you have been missing.

Activities to Heighten Awareness of Appreciative Listening

Activity 1

a)   Do you think you'd benefit from increasing the amount of time you spend on appreciative listening?
b)   What kind of music or other sounds do you find enjoyable?
c)   Do you envision that your preferences will change as you get older—do you think that children, adults, and older adults all enjoy the same listening experiences?

Activity 2
Identify a place where you can go to practice appreciative listening—listening for relaxation and enjoyment.

a)   What sounds are you likely to hear?
b)   If you have a busy schedule, you may have difficulty finding time to just meet your daily commitments. Under these circumstances, how might you increase opportunities to tune in to the relaxing sounds around you?

Activity 3

a)   Do you think appreciative listening is always deliberate and mindful?
b)   Under what circumstances might you engage in appreciative listening without even realizing it?
c)   Given your personality and personal style, what benefits might you expect from this activity?

Assess Your Current Listening Behavior: Hearing

Rate your *hearing* on the following scale of 1 to 5.

_____5. I am able to completely focus my attention on the things that are important and not get distracted. My friends are amazed with my ability to concentrate and the accuracy with which I hear things.

_____4. I can almost always focus my attention on the things that are import-ant. I am successful in avoiding or overcoming distractions and think of myself as someone who hears well.

_____3. I usually focus my attention on the things that are important. At times I get distracted, but I'd say I do as well or better than most people. I'm right about what I hear most of the time.

_____2. I have a hard time concentrating for long periods of time. I think I focus on the things that are important, but sometimes I get distracted and miss important information. There's really nothing wrong with my hearing.

_____1. I'm not great at concentrating. I just get bored, get distracted. My mind wanders easily. I try to focus but then something else attracts my attention. I guess I don't hear everything that is said.

4

LISTEN TO UNDERSTAND

Outcomes

Understanding, or listening comprehension, can easily be taken for granted. Creating shared meanings—ensuring that the message you receive is what the speaker intended—is a complex process, especially in a diverse workplace. You can never be completely sure that you've "got it right" when you listen. Some listening experts have suggested that you are simply making good guesses as you try to understand what the speaker intends, especially in situations where your past experiences, beliefs, and goals are different.

Interruptions are one of the most common barriers to shared meanings. Listeners think they have understood, but often they have only have a portion of the message. They've made assumptions based on their own experiences and stopped the speaker before she could finish her thoughts. While there are a variety of ways to increase the likelihood that you understand what you hear, perception-checking is one of the most effective. Simply repeating the speaker's message and asking for clarification can go a long way toward sharing meanings in all types of challenging circumstances.

While perception-checking is an effective strategy in interpersonal communication situations, understanding a presentation requires a different set of skills. Often, the challenge is to distinguish the speaker's main ideas from the less important details that serve to create interest but that aren't essential to understanding the message. Fortunately, there are a number of things you can do to ensure that the speaker's points are clear.

Listening Outcome U1: Meet the Challenge of Individual Differences

Consider if I said to you, "I was going out to the car and my dog jumped on me!" Now, describe the situation. What did you imagine happened? Was

I dressed in sweats and sneakers? A suit? Was the dog a poodle? A shepherd? Whenever you hear something, you rely heavily on past experiences to give meaning to your vision, to your understanding of the message. Yet, even from this simple example, it's clear that just because you're listening doesn't mean you're really on the same page as the speaker. And, no surprise, the less familiar you are with your partner, and the less you have in common, the more difficult it is to really understand what he means.

Your workplace—your world—is becoming increasingly diverse. You will need to consider your partners' backgrounds, values, and past experiences as you exchange messages and work together. Developments in technology that make zooming across continents so convenient may also lead to the false impression that communication has been effective when, in fact, diversity may have created a situation where meanings are far from aligned. "Let's celebrate!" What does that *mean* to a Texan? An under-represented minority? A German who has only been in the United States for a week? "I got to work really early" may well have a different meaning for individuals with difference experiences and work backgrounds. The bottom line: Never take understanding for granted.

Skills for Success

1. Learn About the Person Speaking
The same message from two different people is likely to have two very different meanings. What variables should you consider when your goal is to make sure you accurately understand a message? Diversity has many dimensions: Age, gender, ethnicity, socio-economic background, education, and so forth. When your goal is effective listening, it's helpful to consider both individual differences and similarities.

2. Recognize Assumptions
There are endless examples of how differences in past experience and individual perceptions can lead to miscommunication. It can be dangerous to "assume" that it's the speaker's responsibility to provide the information you need to get a clear understanding! As a listener, you share responsibility for effective communication. Recognizing what you know, and what you need to know, is a part of your job. Effective communication is not only a shared task —it's helpful if the listener assumes more than half of the responsibility!

3. Check Your Perceptions
Asking questions is an important listener function. When you hear something that confuses you or when you aren't quite sure what the speaker intended, don't hesitate to ask for more background or an explanation. Questions facilitate listening by drawing the speaker out and letting her know you have a genuine interest in what she has to say. You might find yourself thinking,

"That's a silly question," or stop yourself for fear that the speaker will assume you weren't listening. Often, however, confusion results because the speaker did not accurately assess your background and familiarity with the topic, or left out important details, or spoke too quickly. Regardless of the reason, it's your job to make sure that you understand what you hear.

Activities to Recognize the Impact of Individual Differences

Activity 1
When someone meets you for the first time, what might they assume about you? They may get clues from your appearance, your job, or your personal manner.

a)   Write down five possible assumptions.
b)   Then, generate the indicators you believe could be used to form these impressions.
c)   Now, go down the list and determine which are not true. Are there any consequences to people holding beliefs that are inaccurate? Are there any assumptions that affect others' willingness and interest in listening to you?

Activity 2
You will need a partner for this exercise—someone you don't know well. Introduce yourself and then begin by responding to one of the questions below. After your response, allow your partner a chance to clarify by giving you accurate information. In each case, try to identify the basis on which assumptions were made.

   Did you assume that your partner:

1.   had grown up in a small town or a big city?
2.   had come from a large family or a small one?
3.   would rather swim or read?
4.   would enjoy big parties or small social gatherings?
5.   would prefer Mexican or Italian food?

Add your own questions to the list!

Activity 3
How might each of the following individuals view a situation differently?
Situation: A street party

1.   a child
2.   an older resident
3.   a teenage band member

Situation: Grocery shopping

1. a father of three
2. a college student
3. a wheelchair-bound older adult

Situation: Taking a cruise

1. someone who can't swim
2. a teenager
3. someone with a health condition

    a) What conflicts or misunderstandings might arise from one or more of these perceptual differences?

    b) Give an example of when you have been in a situation where your perceptions weren't shared by others. What was it? What happened?

Activity 4

a) What additional challenges in comprehension do you face when you listen on Zoom, cell phones, or other distance technologies?

b) In a small group, brainstorm ways to increase understanding when communication takes place at a distance or over mediated channels.

c) What future challenges do you imagine are in store as we increasingly depend on technology for our communications?

Activity 5

When you want to be very certain that your understanding is correct, one method of checking is to restate the message in your own words and provide your partner with an opportunity to either confirm your understanding or clarify his intent. This is called *perception-checking*.

a) Pair up with a classmate and ask your partner to read the passage below.

    • Tomorrow is a real killer. Jose needs a ride to the airport at 10 am, but I have a big meeting in the afternoon and I'm not sure if I'll be able to get away. At least, I know I'll stress about it. It takes, what, about 45 minutes to get to the airport from here? Or maybe if you are coming from Lincoln Street it's not quite as bad but, either way, I just don't have the time. What would he think if I told him to take a cab? He's a really good friend; I don't want him to feel like I'm neglecting him. Can you help me out?

b) Then, practice restating. Take turns reading and perception-checking.

c) You might also use your own situation in place of these samples and see how well your partner understands your message. Later, when interrupting messages is discussed, you will practice a similar skill called paraphrase. The paraphrase is slightly different as your intent is to capture the speaker's emotions as well as the content of her message.

Check your perceptions. Respond with one clear statement of what your friend wants.

d) Repeat the activity with the passage below.

- Nida was excited about the holiday party she was hosting, but was overwhelmed thinking about all the various activities that needed to be accomplished. You stopped by to see if there was anything she needed. Immediately she began: "I am so glad to see you! Who knew there would be so much to do?! I've got two cakes in the oven; I'm making fudge—the first batch was so hard I had to throw it out—and I just got a call from Sandy, who says that we absolutely need peanut-butter cookies. The kids just got on the bus to school, so they are out of my hair, but the yard is an absolute mess. The tables need to be set up, the toys put away—I can't begin to think about the mess in the house as well!"

Check your perceptions. Respond with one clear statement of how Nida could use your help.

Listening Outcome U2: Learn about Everything You Can

The more knowledgeable you become, the better able you will be to put new ideas into a context and build on what's already familiar to you. But you can't "get smart" unless you are proactive and deliberately work to increase your mental database. This isn't a one-shot deal; it's a way of viewing the world as you develop habits of inquiry. You probably have friends who are perfectly satisfied to keep everything just as it is. They're the ones who get into arguments and, rather than considering new information, focus entirely on defending their own viewpoint. When you deliberately seek alternative ideas and experiences, you will find that you become more open-minded and receptive to new ideas as well.

Skills for Success

1. Ask Questions

The easiest way to gather information is to ask questions. While that might seem easy, framing questions to elicit complete and accurate responses is a learned skill. Inappropriate questions, leading questions, or irrelevant questions

---

BOX 4.1 TYPES OF QUESTIONS

Closed—Ask closed questions when you want a short, direct, and specific response.
"What company did you work for before joining Google?"

Open—Open questions allow your partner alternatives regarding how they respond. There is more than one way to answer the question and, generally, you get more useful information from this type.
"What did you like about working at Google?"

Leading—Your partner can tell from the way you ask the question what you expect, or want, as their response. This type of question creates bias in the information you receive.
"Wasn't Google amazing with all of its employee benefits?"

Probing—There are many types of probes, which are questions that encourage your partner to elaborate on a particular topic. Probes are often useful after your partner has made an initial, often incomplete or superficial, response.
"Tell me more about how Google tries to make work fun."

---

all do more harm than good for the relationship and for your understanding. It's useful to learn how to distinguish among different types of questions. Then, you can apply the most appropriate questioning strategy so that you know your inquiries are helpful and effective.

2. Increase Your Vocabulary
Whatever you're thinking, there's probably a word for it. While you want to seem approachable and not use words that are so esoteric that no one knows what you're talking about, language is an amazing human capacity—and most of us don't begin to realize its potential for expressing ideas. Words really do open the door to more precise and clearer thinking and understanding. That's probably why every culture has continuously created new words. Just think about technology and how, even a very few years ago, no one talked so frequently about social media, e-readers, Zoom, or video streaming. There's an interesting question that linguists debate—whether or not you can actually have a thought for which there is no word. If you can't articulate what is in your mind, how do you even consider the idea? Regardless of your position on the issue, you can see how using a more sophisticated and precise vocabulary will help you listen—and communicate—more effectively.

3. Increase Openness to New Ideas and Information
Do friends describe you as curious? Spontaneous? Flexible? These characteristics are generally associated with open-mindedness, a quality that is critical if

you are to expand your thinking and your understanding. It's difficult to learn new things if you assume you know everything—or, more likely, if you assume that what you think you know is true! There's a quote that many attribute to Mark Twain. It reads, "It ain't what you don't know that gets you into trouble, it's what you know for sure that just ain't so." It's worth pondering, and worth reflecting on whether you approach new situations with enough curiosity and enthusiasm to expand your worldview in beneficial ways.

Activities to Help You Become More Knowledgeable

Activity 1
Attend a seminar or lecture on a topic that is new to you.

a) Was the material difficult to understand? Was the vocabulary unfamiliar?
b) Identify specific ways in which the information you heard might be useful in the future; in other words, give yourself good reasons for listening.

Activity 2
Make a plan to learn a new word every day.

a) Ask your friends who study different subjects to share vocabulary that might be specific to that field. Write down each word you learn for a month.
b) How might you introduce new words into your own conversation?
c) Do your friends use words in sophisticated ways? What would their reaction be if you increased your vocabulary? Why do you think that's the case?
d) How do your peers influence you use of language? How would your vocabulary change in the workplace?

Activity 3
Certain ideas can be expressed in a variety of ways. Take a look at the following sentences and then find at least one other way to express the same message.

Statement	Alternate Expression
1. It's been a long day.	1. *Wow, I can't wait to get home!*
2. I hope I'm chosen next.	2.
3. I don't know what to do.	3.
4. I wonder if she likes me.	4.
5. It's fun to play with pets.	5.
6. Sometimes I can be a real jerk.	6.
7. Awesome!	7.

a) How would you describe the difference between the statement and your alternate expression?
b) Which variation would you be most likely to use with your peers? Your parents?

Activity 4
Find a help-wanted ad that describes a position for which you could apply. Give it to a classmate and ask him to create five interview questions that include at least three different types (refer to Box 4.1). Role play the interview for approximately five minutes. Ask the interviewer to write down the most insightful and useful information obtained. Discuss the interaction.

a) What type of questions were asked?
b) Which questions yielded the most useful information?
c) Were all questions appropriate?
d) What else would you ask if you could create another question?

Activity 5
Think about the type of questions you ask and the situations in which you're most likely to pose a question. Rate yourself on the following scale.

	Never	*Seldom*	*Sometimes*	*Usually*	*Always*
a. I give my partner time to think after I ask a question.	1	2	3	4	5
b. I am tactful in asking questions.	1	2	3	4	5
c. I hesitate to ask questions that are personal.	1	2	3	4	5
d. I probe a lot, using questions to understand a topic in greater depth.	1	2	3	4	5
e. I feel like I'm holding up the conversation when I ask questions.	1	2	3	4	5
f. I'm annoyed by people who ask too many questions.	1	2	3	4	5
g. I'm known as the person with all the questions.	1	2	3	4	5

Activity 6
Do you think of yourself as someone who is curious?

a) List ten things that you'd like to learn more about.
b) What might prevent you from asking questions? Consider both physical (too far from the speaker) and psychological (afraid it would sound stupid) reasons.
c) Select three items on your list and identify specific actions you can take to find out more about each. Decide where to begin!

Listening Outcome U3: Zero In on Key Points

Speakers tend to get caught up in details, whether speaking to large groups, to friends in a coffee shop, or chatting online. At the end of the day, if you sit back, there may be many instances where it will be difficult for you to determine what the "take-aways" were from your exchange. In other words, what did you really learn or discover? What was the point? This is a good question because studies at more than one major university discovered that students didn't really understand the point of the lectures. They were asked to listen to a guest speaker and told they would be tested on what they heard during the following class. They came in prepared—prepared to recite lists and describe theories and name key concepts that were presented. What they couldn't do was to explain the speaker's point—they were unsure of the purpose of the lecture and couldn't answer questions such as, "Why did the speaker choose this subject?" and "How is the information useful?"

Skills for Success

1. Take Notes; Distinguish Main Points from Evidence and Support
There are many people who say they don't see the point of taking notes. If you are among them, it's time to change! Taking notes is essential if you want to understand and use the information you hear, because what you learn matters. Oral messages are fleeting and often disorganized. The only way to reflect on what you hear is by capturing it in notes, whether you have a pen or a keyboard. As you record a message, you can impose a structure that will help

---

BOX 4.2 COMMON PATTERNS OF ORGANIZATION

Organizational patterns help you as a listener understand and make sense of what you hear. The pattern refers to the relationship among the main points; each main idea is then "developed" with additional examples, facts, statistics, and other material.

Chronological—Main points follow a time sequence.

Topical—Main points are equal in importance and scope, and can be placed in any order.

Order of importance or complexity—A variation of topical; points sequenced by importance, complexity, or another pattern.

Spatial—Main points are organized around a location or relative position.

Problem/solution—First a problem is described in detail, followed by one or more recommendations for how it might be resolved.

Reasons—A persuasive organization that involves clearly defining a position or proposition, and then providing reasons or arguments in support.

you differentiate the main points from the evidence. Note-taking also helps you to figure out the significance and relevance of the information you hear. There are several simple patterns of organization. Using any one of them will help you impose additional structure on what might be random and jumbled thoughts, and better understand the key ideas.

2. Clarify Conversations

When you're engaged in a conversation, you might feel awkward taking notes. You might think it's inappropriate or even rude. Yet, you still need to ensure that you understand the speaker's main message, regardless of how engaging her stories and personal experiences may be. In fact, some speakers become so engaged in the details of their story that it will be up to you to bring the conversation back to the main point. Why is she telling you this? It's interesting that her grandmother was still hang-gliding at 80, but the point? As a listener, you need to ensure that effective communication takes place in whatever way you can.

3. Determine the Main Purpose When Listening to Social Media and Mediated Communication

It really doesn't matter where you are getting your information; listening still requires that you organize and make sense of what you hear. The process of listening to mediated communication is so different from listening in interpersonal contexts that it takes a separate set of skills. Social media often bombards listeners with fragmented messages, making it particularly important that you impose some order to determine what is important for you to know. This activity takes practice; you can't expect to catch everything the first time around. If you believe the message may be important, however, you'll need to figure out what is central and what is simply there to grab your attention. In some cases there is a secondary message, and it's important to be aware of how both are affecting you. For instance, while it might appear that you are listening to a straightforward message on YouTube, the sender may also be hoping to communicate her extensive knowledge and credibility on the subject.

Activities to Help You Focus on Key Points

Activity 1

When you are engaged in a conversation, you can always check your understanding by restating what you believe to be the speaker's key points.

a)   During the next two days, create opportunities to practice restating the speaker's main points and write down what you think are the key ideas.
b)   Check with the speaker to see if you were correct. Make it a habit to always ask yourself, "What is the speaker's purpose?" and "What is the main point she is trying to make?"

Activity 2
Get together with several classmates and select one of the topics below.

a)   Decide what you want to say about the subject and create a position statement.
b)   Generate three main points you could make about one of the subjects.
c)   Take each point separately and brainstorm the supporting information you might use. It's fine to make it up!
d)   Look at the difference between the main point and the facts, examples, or other development you have used to support or clarify the idea.

Example: Cats
Position statement: Cats make good pets.
Points:

1.   Cats are low-maintenance and easy to care for.
2.   Cats are friendly.
3.   Cats are inexpensive.

Supporting information for point 1.

•   You can leave a cat overnight.
•   Cats don't need to be walked.
•   Cats will sleep almost anywhere.

Additional topics:
a.   laptops
b.   the student services office
c.   calculus
d.   the pizza place

Activity 3
Review the various patterns of organization (see Box 4.2).

a)   Create a presentation outline for three of the topics listed below. In each case, follow a specific organizational structure (chronological, order of importance, and so forth). Apply a different pattern for each of the three topics you select. Notice that the purpose of some topics is to persuade, while others are intended to inform.

     •   Laptops should come in more colors.
     •   How to select the best tablet for your needs.
     •   Activities of the student services office.
     •   Every student should take advantage of the student services office.
     •   Why calculus is so difficult for most people.

- No one should be required to take calculus.
- How the pizza place created its unique ambience.
- The pizza place restaurant is over-rated.

b) When you're finished, hand your work to one of your classmates to review. See if they can identify the pattern you have applied in each case.

Listening Outcome U4: Reduce Interruptions

There are few things that block accurate understanding more than interruptions. However, some interruptions, like stopping the speaker to ask for clarification, are important listening behaviors. If you are confused by something that's said, your mind will linger, trying to figure out what the speaker is talking about. During those few seconds when you're reflecting on a past comment, you won't be listening; when you try to pick up where you left off, you're likely to find that you're now missing important pieces of the message. The more confused you feel, the less likely you are to be able to recover until, inevitably, you give up entirely on understanding and resort to just nodding and smiling! In most cases, it's far better to interrupt with a question that allows the speaker to clarify or elaborate—and then move on. In those more formal situations where interrupting is disruptive or inappropriate, write your question down so that you can get clarification at a later time.

Most people, however, don't interrupt for clarification. One of the most common reasons for interrupting is to change the focus of the conversation to yourself. The speaker is explaining what he thinks about a laptop that's just hit the market; then, without hesitation, you chime in with your opinion. The speaker is describing her hectic weekend; you interject with the details of how crazy busy you've been with the arrival of your relatives and the paper that was due and the tickets you had to a Saturday game. While it's good to let the speaker know you share some of the same thoughts and feelings that she's expressing, taking the focus away and moving on with your personal experiences can block understanding. In some cases, behaviors that are seen as insensitive or self-serving even lead to a strained relationship. Of course, your communication partner may be interested in your adventures, but let her finish before you tell your stories.

Skills for Success

1. Keep the Focus On Your Partner, Let Go of Your Personal Agenda
A common reason why many people say they interrupt is that they are afraid if they don't speak that very second, they will forget what they wanted to say. Could their ideas be *that* important? Their assumption is, of course, that nothing

the speaker says is going to change their ideas or point of view—and that getting their thoughts across is helping the conversation in some essential way. While this is sometimes the case, more often than not the "listener" is simply not listening... he is anxious to be the speaker and to interject his own ideas into the conversation, hoping to impress everyone with his knowledge or experience. In most cases this person's mental energy has been spent on creating his own message rather than on trying to understand what the other person is saying. The solution? It's not easy to break longstanding habits like interrupting, but you can start with an understanding of the conditions when you generally interrupt. Then make a firm commitment to modify your behavior.

2. Monitor Your Own Behavior
You can do it—you can learn to reduce the number of times you interrupt when someone else is speaking. First, be honest—is this a goal you really want to accomplish? Because you can't change a habit unless you are willing to put in the effort required and get the help you need.

What are friends for? If you spend a significant amount of time with another person, let them know that you want to be "signaled" whenever you interrupt. You can't change a behavior unless you are aware every time it occurs. Soon, you will begin to recognize when you are interrupting and be able to identify the circumstances under which it is most likely to happen. Perhaps you become impatient when someone speaks slowly, or get too emotionally involved when discussing certain topics. In any case, simply recognizing the behavior when it happens is prerequisite to making it stop!

3. Use Self-Talk
Some of the same techniques you applied to help with concentration will also help you keep from interrupting. One of these is what we call "self-talk," the process of directing your extra mental "thought time" so that you can use it in productive ways. If you keep your mental energies focused on your listening task, you will be surprised at how much more information you can gain from a conversation or presentation.

Activities to Reduce Interruptions

Activity 1
For at least a week, keep track of the number of times you interrupt someone as well as the times someone interrupts you. Note who was speaking, what the topic was, and any other information that would help you assess the reasons why the interruption occurred.

a) Do you interrupt some people more than others? Why would that be the case?
b) Who interrupts you? What is your relationship with the person?

c) Are there circumstances you can identify that make it more likely that interruptions might occur?

d) What might you do to avoid or reduce the dysfunctional interruptions?

Activity 2

Relate a personal experience to some of your classmates. Choose something you enjoy talking about.

a) As you speak, others in the group will take turns interrupting you and turning the focus to their own ideas and experiences.

b) After two to three minutes, discuss the results.

- How did these interruptions make you feel?
- How did those who were interrupting feel about their role?
- Would have it had the same effect if you had been talking about something less personal?

Activity 3

Sometimes people don't realize that they are interrupting, or they rationalize and defend their behavior.

a) Under what circumstances do you personally believe is it okay to interrupt?

b) Do you think everyone is capable of reducing or stopping self-focused interruptions?

c) What would happen if everyone interrupted, all the time?!

d) Do you think interrupting is a learned behavior? Is it cultural?

Activity 4

You probably talk to yourself more than you realize. The problem is that much of your "self-talk" is about things you anticipate or are reflecting on that have little to do with the conversation at hand! Using self-talk to improve your comprehension requires that you repeat the message you are hearing and deliberately keep your current conversation the center of your attention.

a) Review the suggestions in Chapter 3, Box 3.1, which address the value of self-talk (Vocalized Listening Technique). While self-talk is useful both in conversations and when listening to presentations, comprehension is generally more difficult when communication is one-way.

b) The next time you listen to a lecture or presentation, deliberately try to follow the guidelines of self-talk and answer the following questions.

- What self-talk strategies did you apply?
- What challenges emerged as you worked to better focus and understand the message?

- What will you do differently next time you use self-talk in a presentation or lecture situation?

Assess Your Current Listening Behavior: Understanding

Rate your *understanding* on the following scale of 1 to 5.

_____5. I always recognize the impact of individual differences on listening and take these into consideration. I'm also really good at identifying the main points when someone speaks. I can keep myself from interrupting because I enjoy learning about new things.

_____4. I'm sensitive to the impact of individual differences on listening. I work to identify the main points when someone speaks, and I don't have any problem keeping the focus on the speaker and not interrupting because I like to hear other people's ideas.

_____3. I usually take individual differences into account when I listen. I also catch myself if I focus on details rather than a speaker's main point. I like to learn about new things, although I probably interrupt more than I should.

_____2. It's not unusual for me to be in the middle of a conversation before I remember that individual differences have an impact on listening. I guess you could call me a talker, because the truth is I would rather be telling a story than listening to one.

_____1. I never thought individual differences were a big deal. I'm not sure how I would change anything as a result. I listen to the things that interest me, and I can usually figure out the speaker's main point. If I interrupt, I always have a good reason.

5

LISTEN TO REMEMBER

Outcomes

Remembering is essential in order for you to apply what you have heard at a later time. It's hard to imagine someone being described as an effective listener if, as soon as they hear something, they completely forget what was said! They would likely be perceived as someone who doesn't follow through, who can't be trusted to keep their promises. You have a better chance of remembering if you use both your visual and your auditory senses. There are many types of both short- and long-term memory techniques that enable you to store information in ways that make it easy to recall it when you need to use it. A range of personal factors, as well as stress, can affect your ability to remember. Keep in mind, however, that when you apply effective memory strategies your ability to recall is virtually unlimited; if you store information properly, the more you have in your memory "files," the more associations you can make to retrieve the information you need.

Listening Outcome R1: Recognize Individual Factors that Affect Memory

Have you ever compared your memory to that of your friends or family? Often, someone will get a reputation for having a great memory—you might find yourself saying, "Ask Shannon. She'll remember!" It's true that basic individual differences affect your competence and potential; your memory is influenced by personal characteristics and other factors inherent in the particular communication situation. But, if you think other people remember things more readily than you do, don't give up! There are a variety of things you can do to improve your memory—and a number of variables over which you have complete control that make remembering easy or difficult. One thing you'll discover is that there are a lot of people who would like to have a better memory, and a lot of employers out there who value this ability.

Perhaps the easiest way to think about memory is to divide it into short-term and long-term processes. If your goal is to remember something just long enough to use it—a phone number, a shopping list, the name of your dentist, the room where a test will be given—then short-term techniques will be helpful.

If the information you hear is important, something that you want to remember indefinitely, then you'll find that long-term memory strategies provide a basis for building storage files in your mind. Of course, obstacles to remembering can appear at any time. It's good to know what to look out for so you can anticipate and reduce memory blocks. Before you go any further, keep one more thing in mind—improving your memory takes patience, persistence, and work!

Skills for Success

1. Take Age and Gender into Account When You Listen
Think of age as the bell curve of listening. While most young children have very short attention spans and remember little of what was said from one day to the next, older adults have other reasons why they don't remember as well as they once did.

A consistent, calm message to children regarding respectful behavior is probably the most effective path to preparing them for later listening situations. Get their attention, create relatively short messages, and always help them understand how they are going to use the information they hear. Keep your expectations in line with their abilities or you run the risk of causing stress and interfering with memory still further.

Most older adults not only have some degree of hearing loss, but may also suffer from anxiety, the effects of medications, or traumatic life events. It is particularly important, then, that you listen with patience and understand the memory challenges they may encounter. In many cases, it becomes more difficult for an older adult to recall things from the immediate past. In addition, it becomes difficult for seniors to use the memory strategies available because, if information has not been stored properly, it is not as readily available for retrieval. Given the range of memory issues seniors may experience, one effective approach is storytelling. Storytelling links information in much the same way as memory devices and can be comforting as it helps individuals to further connect with family and friends.

2. Recognize Personal Characteristics that Influence Listening
Recognizing your limitations and your potential is an important step in memory improvement. It's easy to make excuses for why you "can't

remember," and even to begin to label yourself as someone with a "poor memory." Like other aspects of the listening process, a positive attitude and self-efficacy are essential to making progress. While high intelligence, natural curiosity, and other personal attributes may influence how difficult it is for you to remember something, there's really no reason why you can't improve your memory with concentrated practice and a basic understanding of the memory principles involved.

Activities to Recognize Personal Factors that Affect Memory

Activity 1
There are a lot of changes that take place with aging. One of the most significant has to do with what and how much an individual remembers.

a) Talk with at least one older adult—someone aged over 80 years if possible. Ask them what they notice about their memory and if there are any techniques they use to help them better remember daily activities.
b) Ask an older adult about their past experiences, things that happened when they were much younger. Most older adults can vividly recall things that happened years ago, but have trouble with more short-term requirements.
c) Keep notes on your conversation and your subsequent observations. Share them with your classmates.

Activity 2
Story-telling is an amazing method of not only helping older adults recall the past, but also of showing genuine interest in what someone has to say. Helping an older person connect with past life experiences often enables them to remember additional events and details.

a) Identify a relative or friend who is an older adult. Rather than asking them to provide details about an event, pose a more general, open-ended question. Inquire about an experience in their lives. You are likely to have most success if you simply provide a catalyst that encourages them to "tell the story."
b) Report back to your class on what you discovered.

Activity 3
Men and women remember different things, often because of their gender-linked interests. As you know, we tend to pay attention to those things that are important to us, and this focus influences what gets into our memory systems.

a)   Divide a group of classmates or friends into separate teams of men and women.
b)   Ask the women to generate a list of items or topics they think men remember better than they do.
c)   Do the same for the group of men.
d)   Share lists and have the men react to the items on the list the women generated, and vice versa.
e)   What are the assumptions that were made about the "other" gender?
f)   How accurate were they?

Activity 4
What other factors affect someone's memory besides age and gender?

a)   With a group of classmates, brainstorm a list of individual variables you believe influence someone's ability to remember.
b)   Identify at least two or three of the items that you think apply to *your* memory.

Activity 5
It's helpful to reflect on your own memory as you work to improve this listening skill.

a)   Do you consider yourself to be good at remembering things?
b)   What specific behaviors or personal characteristics contribute to your ability to remember?
c)   What contributes to difficulties you experience with memory?
d)   What would be some of the specific advantages to you personally of having an improved memory? Given your anticipated career, how can a better memory help you on the job?

Listening Outcome R2: Remember Names and Other Short-Term Memory Information

Can't remember? There is something you can do about it, and the time it takes to improve your memory is time well spent. The first step is to identify the situations in which you have the most difficulty, because each memory breakdown has a different cause and a different remedy.

Let's first talk about the things you don't want to remember forever—things you want to hold in your memory just long enough to accomplish the task. In this category would be your grocery list or that phone number you need to put into your speed dial. Perhaps you're hosting a small group of friends and are trying to remember which beverage they said they'd like with their meal. As you become more aware of what we call short-term memory, you'll likely discover that you are depending on this skill many times a day. The question is, are you good at it? Do you readily remember what you hear?

Think about the specific things you do when you're in the car and someone gives you directions. You can't write anything down; you just have to remember it—turns, street names, the number of blocks. Now imagine that you're in a hurry. You're late for a doctor's appointment or trying to get to a party before the ice cream in your shopping bag melts. Stress contributes to disrupting your concentration, and your memory. Suddenly you're not sure just what directions you were given. You turn to your passenger and impatiently ask her how many blocks before the turn. She gives you a look and says, "I'm not driving. I wasn't listening."

Skills for Success

1. Keep Focused on the Message
It's impossible to remember something that you never heard. You've probably been introduced to someone only to stress out because you didn't remember the name. It's probably not that you forgot it—more likely, you never caught it in the first place because you were thinking about what you were going to say next or about what your new acquaintance was thinking about your new suit. In any case, your focus was on yourself rather than on the person you met. Imagine you are at a reception and are called over to a small group to be introduced. What are you thinking? "I need to really concentrate on these names"? Or, more likely, "What will I say? How do I look? I hope I don't have bad breath"! When you're thinking primarily about yourself, it's no surprise that you have trouble remembering. And this doesn't happen just with introductions. It's important, then, to be more mindful of where your attention is focused. Worrying about others' perceptions can prevent you from listening and remembering what you hear.

2. Use Memory Devices: Repetition, Chunking, Logical Patterns
Do you want to improve your short-term memory? Just ask! There are numerous self-help strategies available and stories (almost all true!) about how someone just like you applied short-term memory principles to realize amazing results. Two of the easiest memory techniques are *repetition* and *chunking*.

With *repetition*, you simply keep repeating the information you need to remember until you get a chance to use it. *Chunking* means that, instead of trying to recall discrete pieces of information, you create a mental link that will enable you to remember fewer "pieces." If you have a grocery list, for instance, you might put bananas, oranges, and a melon under "fruit"—or coffee, oatmeal, and toast under "breakfast." By creating categories and finding a logic behind the seemingly unrelated items, you can make connections among almost any seemingly unrelated pieces of information—and remember them. If you need a more concrete goal, most research suggests that you should easily be able to link up to seven unrelated items. Of course, you can always try for more!

Activities to Improve Short-Term Memory and Name Recall

Activity 1
Are there situations in which you already use a short-term memory technique? If so, what is it? Identify other situations where such an aid would come in handy.

Activity 2
Form a group with several of your classmates.

a) Create an eight–item list of words—anything that comes to mind. A sample list is provided below.
Potatoes, poodles, canoe, eraser, broom, notebook, paint, socks.

b) Take turns reading the list to other members of your group, pausing for a second in between items. Group members then practice applying repetition or chunking as a memory device.

c) Then, ask group members to respond to the following questions (use the ones below or make up your own).

   1) What was the fourth word?
   2) What letter did the second word begin with?
   3) What word came just before _____?
   4) What was the next-to-last item?

Repeat this activity with at least three different lists. You might try numbers instead of words; some people can remember one type of information much more easily than another.

After completing the exercise, respond to the following questions.

1. What words are easiest for you to remember?
2. Which short-term memory technique did you use to recall the items?
3. Were some items easier or harder for different group members to recall?
4. What short-term memory strategy would work best for you in this situation?

Activity 3
Form a six- to eight-member team.

a. Make up a history or "bio" for yourself—a new name, job title, family, and so forth. Write down the new information to use later.

b.   Introduce yourself to the rest of the group. Classmates try to focus their attention and remember your profile without taking any notes.

c.   Draw names randomly to form pairs. Introduce your partner to the rest of the group and include as much of the information they presented as you can recall.

Activity 4
Examine the following lists.

1)   Table, fruit, fork, cup, apple, soda, coffee.
2)   Dog, horse, pig, spider, nail, water, hay.
3)   Toothpaste, comb, shoes, soap, money, mirror, shaving cream.

   a)   Determine how you would use chunking as a short-term memory device in each case.

   b)   Share your strategies with your classmates. Did anyone create a particularly effective method of chunking?

Listening Outcome R3: Improve Your Long-Term Memory

There are numerous occasions where you may be listening to information that you will need to use at a later time—information that you'd like to have access to whenever you need it. In classes, the concepts you learn often link to later material. In your job—whether counseling, managing, teaching, selling, or something else—others depend on you to recall and apply what you've heard. You wouldn't want a doctor to say to you, "I just heard about that new medicine at a conference last week but, darn, I don't recall what it will do to you!"

You will benefit from developing your long-term memory so that you can readily store and accurately retrieve information. While a number of factors influence how and what you remember—and how much difficulty you have retrieving the information you heard—applying the skills below will make a big difference. And, the more information you put into your long-term memory, the more "mental files" you create and the easier it is to store new information in ways that allow you to retrieve it. You've probably heard that when something new goes in one ear, something old goes out the other— NOT true! If you store information properly, it will always be there to use.

Skills for Success

1. Use Visualization and Imagery
When you want to remember something, don't just think in terms of the words—visualize what you are hearing. Two sensory stimuli are much better

than one when it comes to your long-term memory. If someone says, "Don't forget to pick up the cat at the vet," your best bet is to visualize the cat waiting patiently for you to come and rescue her (or maybe you see her running frantically around the waiting room!). Think of visualization as your "mental theatre," and practice using two channels whenever you need to remember what you hear. The more vivid your image, the more likely you are to retrieve it when it's needed. In addition, putting objects into action or exaggerating the number of items will help your recall. If you want to remember to wear a jacket because it's snowing, visualize standing in your bathing suit in a field with millions of huge snowflakes falling around you. The more senses you can stimulate, the better chance you have of remembering the experience.

2. Why Not Try Mnemonics?
A mnemonic, also known as a memory aid, is a tool that helps you remember an idea or phrase with a pattern of letters, numbers, or other deliberate associations. Mnemonic devices include special rhymes and poems, acronyms, images, songs, outlines, and other memory tools. Types of mnemonics range from simple catchphrases to the creation of abbreviations and rhymes.

Any structure you can impose on the ideas or items you want to put in your memory will help you recall them later. While you may occasionally feel that trying to remember one concept is confounding things you already know, remember, again, that by deliberately linking new information to what is already in your memory system you make all the information easier to retrieve.

Another way to remember information over a period of time is by deliberately making it meaningful. How do you make sense out of nonsense? Review the suggestions in Box 5.1 and see if you can create examples of some of the techniques that are described.

BOX 5.1 A FEW LONG-TERM MEMORY STRATEGIES

- Create a nonsense word out of the first letters of the items you need to recall. For example, yard, airplane, football, and pancakes. Say it several times—pafy, pafy, pafy.
- Link the items you want to remember with a common feature or idea. You're going to the grocery store to get dish detergent, root beer, and olive oil. What do these have in common? You can begin with the fact that they are all liquids.
- Create a story that includes all the items you want to remember. The more outrageous the story, the easier it will be for you to recall. Your items are paper, band aids, soap, and motor oil; you envision a room

with paper all over the floor, some pieces held together with band aids. As you enter the room, you slip on the soap and fall into a pail of motor oil.

- You can better recall items if the information is in an easier-to-recall form. The planets? Try: My Very Excited Mother Just Served Us Nine Pies (Mercury, Venus, Earth, Mars, Jupiter, Saturn, Uranus, Neptune, and Pluto). You may know the lines and spaces in music (EGBDF) correspond to "Every Good Boy Does Fine," or that "Thirty days has September, April, June, and November."

Activities to Improve Your Long-Term Memory

Activity 1

a) Either alone or with some of your classmates, generate a list of the associations you've learned to help improve your memory.

b) Share your list with other members of your class and select the ones you think are most useful.

Activity 2

a) Create a "story" that links items from one of the lists below. Begin with "Once upon a time..."

- tree, snow, computer, tape, steak, bear, carrots
- boat, pink, movie, nail polish, cell phone, door, mail box

b) Practice by creating your own lists and accompanying stories until the process becomes almost automatic.

Activity 3

a) Take the items from Activity 2 and mentally place them as you walk through a familiar setting. Perhaps you open your front door and see a turtle sitting on the TV. You walk into the room and find a horse chewing on your lamp and a hamburger on the shelf. See what you can do!

b) In the next class period, test yourself to see just how much you remembered!

Activity 4

Examine the list in the table below and form a mental picture of each item.

Ease of Visualization (1–5)		Similarity (S or D)
a) _____	A goat in Switzerland	_____
b) _____	A navy ship	_____
c) _____	A tornado	_____
d) _____	A well being drilled	_____
e) _____	Backpacking in the mountains	_____
f) _____	A homemade sailboat	_____
g) _____	Looking down on a city from 40 floors above	_____
h) _____	A rainforest	_____
i) _____	A helicopter in the desert	_____
j) _____	Fjords in Norway	_____
k) _____	A loveable dog	_____
l) _____	A liberal education	_____
m) _____	A major winter traffic jam	_____

a) Which are easiest for you to visualize? Why do you think that's the case?
b) Determine which images you think will probably be very similar among group members and which you think are likely to be quite dissimilar. Again, how did you come to these conclusions?
c) After completing this exercise, discuss the implications of what you discovered.

Rate each item on a scale of 1 to 5 (1—impossible to visualize; 2—difficult to visualize; 3—can visualize; 4—easy to visualize; 5—can visualize quickly and easily). Guess in advance whether your classmates will visualize each image in the same way you do, or whether their mental pictures will be quite different. Indicate "S" for similar, or "D" for different.

Listening Outcome R4: Reduce the Factors that Negatively Affect Memory

Sometimes people can get so stressed that they don't stop to realize how stressed they are! Stress affects many things, and listening is clearly one of them. Emotions in general interfere with your ability to listen and process information objectively. If you are worried, anxious, or even excited, your listening is affected. Stress, however, can be more long-term and more difficult to address.

Recognizing symptoms of stress, and then taking deliberate action to reduce this emotional block, is key to listening well (see Box 5.2). This sounds easy, but finding those 10 to 15 minutes every day to focus on stress reduction takes commitment and determination.

BOX 5.2 RECOGNIZE SIGNS OF STRESS

Physical Signs
Elevated blood pressure and heart rate
Difficulty breathing
Queasy stomach and tight muscles
Back and head pain
Sweating

Emotional Signs
Anxiety and nervousness
Anger and frustration
Depression
Fatigue
Moodiness and Irritability
Worry

Mental Signs
Difficulty concentrating
Poor task performance
Defensiveness
Sleepiness
Mental blocks

Behavioral Signs
Overeating or loss of appetite
Impulsive or aggressive outbursts
Restlessness
Withdrawal
Accident proneness

Organizational Signs
Job burnout
Low morale
Absenteeism and high turnover
Poor performance
Accidents
Poor working relationships

Skills for Success

1. Reduce Stress

Sit quietly. Breathe. Tense your muscles and then release them. Well? Can you feel some tension? Can you distinguish the difference between how your body normally feels and what it's like to relax? Take time every day to do something that allows you to get in touch with your stress and then to relax both your mind and your body.

When you know you are going into a particularly stressful situation, it's good to anticipate the problem and work to reduce stress before it even begins. Take a walk. Exercise. Meditate. Take a shower. Find something that works for you and apply your stress reduction techniques to improve your listening in anxiety-producing situations. Remember that the stress you experience is largely in your mind—everyone experiences the same situations in a slightly different way, and every situation affects each person's listening ability to a different degree. Your goal is to take control of your stress through positive thinking by becoming what we call an active stress manager (see Box 5.3). While a certain amount of stress is good—it keeps you energized and motivated—your goal is to find a balance that enables you to focus and keep your perspective.

2. Overcome Listening Apprehension

Realizing that you are in an important listening situation can cause stress, and that type of stress is called "listening apprehension." Try to identify at least

---

BOX 5.3 BECOME AN ACTIVE STRESS MANAGER

Active Stress Manager	Passive Stress Victim
1. Puts energy into areas that can be managed.	1. Leaves things to chance.
2. Anticipates and plans for the future.	2. Does not think too far ahead.
3. Focuses on high priorities.	3. Works on whatever is going on at the moment.
4. Takes measures to stay healthy.	4. Lets personal and health problems accumulate.
5. Seeks support and relationships.	5. Keeps to self, works independently.
6. Adapts a clear strategy to reduce stress.	6. Feels like a stress victim much of the time.

two specific situations where you feel anxious about your listening requirements. Anxiety, of course, makes it difficult or impossible for you to listen
well. The first thing to do is to take the focus off of yourself and how well
you need to listen and instead focus on the speaker. The key to reducing listening apprehension is to stop thinking about yourself and "how you'll do" as
a listener, and work to put what you hear into a context that makes sense in
light of the speaker and situation.

3. Reduce Overload

Every day you are bombarded with bits of information—sounds and sights that
make your life hectic and stressful and make listening particularly difficult.
Think of all the stimulation you get through the media. The sheer amount of
information, all of the choices and decisions, have a significant impact on your
health and well-being. If you set aside time to engage in other types of activities you will notice a difference in your stress level and your ability to enjoy
the things around you. Spending time with friends and family is particularly
important as you reflect on your priorities and lifestyle.

4. Increase Your Creativity

You'll also discover that as you increase your creativity, your ability to use
long-term memory strategies increases as well. While creating associations and
applying other memory techniques may feel awkward at first, practice and
repetition will help you make these mental strategies a habit. Without doubt
the more comfortable you are with the creative process and the more often
you apply creativity to your mental activities, the easier it will be for you to
quickly remember what you heard.

Activities to Reduce the Factors that Negatively Affect Memory

Activity 1
Do you see yourself as someone who manages stress, or someone who falls
victim to stress on a regular basis? Staying in tune with your body and emotions is important to your health.

a)   Keep notes on when you feel most stressed. Ask yourself questions such as:
  1) what were you doing?
  2) who else was involved?
  3) are there past experiences or beliefs that contribute to your feelings of
      stress?
  4) does this type of situation always cause discomfort?

b)   Then, determine if there are any actions you can take to reduce the stress
     before it affects your mental health and your performance. Select some

behaviors of an active stress manager to reframe the situation and to take control of your response.

Activity 2
Form a group and encourage each person to respond to each of the following questions with the first thing that comes to mind.

1) My most common signs of stress are...
2) Just before encountering a stressful situation, I calm myself by...
3) Listening situations that cause me stress include...
4) Speaking situations that I find stressful include...
5) I know when I am stressed because...
6) The last time I was in a stressful listening situation, I...
7) I could become a more active stress manager by...
8) Self-talk can be either positive or negative in stressful situations; I usually...

    a) Which responses surprised you?
    b) Which responses tended to be very similar to your own?

Activity 3
Identify two specific situations from your past where you have experienced listening apprehension. Then, respond to the accompanying questions.

a) Describe the situation in detail. Who was the speaker? What is your relationship with that person?
b) Can you take the speaker's ideas at face value, or are there aspects that might be distorted or omitted?
c) Reflect: What about the situation made you feel apprehensive? When did you begin to recognize this feeling? What did you do? What was the result—how well did you listen?
d) What could you have done to reduce your apprehension before the occasion? How about during the communication itself?
e) What might you do to confirm that your listening was effective?

Activity 4
Think for a moment about how you regularly express your creativity.

a) Do you think of yourself as creative?
b) Do you notice any recurring blocks to your creativity? These may be related to your environment, your role or situation, other individuals, and even your attitudes.

c) If you know of blocks, what actions might you take to overcome one or more of them?
d) Discuss your ideas with members of a group and share your "best practices."

Activity 5

a) As a member of a group, select one of the items listed below.
    Paper cup, paper clip, keyboard, tape, pen, keys.
b) Take four minutes and brainstorm as many uses for the item as possible (not including its regular function).
c) At the end of the time period, count up your team's ideas and compare to other teams. The team who generated the most items then reads them to the entire class.
d) After the activity, ask yourself the following questions.

   1) Did you feel awkward or energized by this activity?
   2) Did you contribute substantially to the list?
   3) Did you notice any blocks to your creativity? If so, what were they?

Activity 6

Your team has five minutes to be as creative as possible and produce a name, design a logo, and choose a mascot. At the end of the time, each group shares its decisions with the rest of the class.

a) Discuss the process your group used to generate ideas and determine which idea was most creative.
b) Was there one person in your group who came up with suggestions most readily? Was there anyone who didn't contribute any ideas?
c) While most members were focusing on talking—on generating ideas for the assignment—who was listening? How do you know?

Assess Your Current Listening Behavior: Remembering

Rate your *remembering* on the following scale of 1 to 5.

_____5. One of my strengths is my memory. Everyone says they're jealous because I seem to be able to remember both short- and long-term. I recognize that individual factors contribute to this skill, and I am particularly sensitive to how these variables influence my ability to remember.

_____4. I'm pretty good at remembering things, and I'm pretty accurate. My short-term memory is good enough that I'm confident when someone gives me directions or asks me to pick something up. Sure, there are some things I don't remember but most of the time I can come up with the right answers.

_____3. Memory is important, and I think I'm about average at both short- and long-term memory. I can remember most things unless I'm nervous or if it's something that confuses me. I'm certainly as good as most of my friends.

_____2. I don't think about my memory much. I can't say that I'm concerned about it, although there are quite a few times when I've wished I could remember things and I just don't—or, I find out I was wrong.

_____1. I'm good at a lot of things, but memory is definitely not one of them. It's embarrassing sometimes that I forget so quickly and so often. I don't think it's that I don't care... I just can't remember.

6

LISTEN TO INTERPRET

Outcomes

When you listen to interpret what you hear, you go beyond the speaker's words and take into account other important elements of the message. You try to understand the person speaking as well as the context in which communication takes place. To accomplish this, you need to demonstrate both perceptive and behavioral empathy. First, you observe the total communication situation and focus on the speaker's nonverbal behaviors so that you recognize, and can then consider, the emotional component of the message. You try to find out as much as you can about the context—what other factors might be influencing the speaker's attitudes or position on the topic? Each person's background and past experiences dramatically influence his or her reactions. What are the speaker's motives? Beliefs? Fears? Second, empathic listeners develop behavioral empathy; they let their partner know, through both their behavior and their words, that he or she has been understood. Your eye contact, facial expression, tone of voice, and even your posture all send messages about the quality of your listening.

Listening Outcome 11: Develop Cognitive Empathy by Recognizing Individual Differences

Empathy, as you know, most often refers to your ability and willingness to take the role of another person and to try to see things from their point of view. If you think someone is being unreasonable when you hear them ask for a refund, for instance, empathy would enable you to take the other person's perspective and imagine what it would be like to have very little money and then to find the product you purchased didn't work. Effective listeners are socially sensitive—they recognize individual differences and work to understand not only the words but the person speaking. They continue to observe the speaker and attend to cues that help them determine how to respond. The other person's culture, gender, age, and life experiences influence how they see the world. Your job is to become sensitive to the cues that help you recognize different perspectives and then accurately interpret what you hear.

Skills for Success

1. Recognize the Importance of Attitudes
Only when you are open-minded are you in a position to really understand and empathize with another person and his or her situation. Attitudes are difficult to self-identify—very few of us would say we were biased, unfair, or lacked perspective! Yet, everyone sees the world through the lens of their personal and unique past experiences and culture. Overcoming this obstacle to effective listening is difficult. It takes consistent effort to recognize the attitudes that might be preventing you from putting yourself in the other person's position.

2. Recognize and Account for Cultural and Demographic Differences
It is particularly difficult to empathize when you have little knowledge of the other person's culture or life experiences. Can you empathize with a friend who has a serious hangover if you don't drink? How much empathy would you have for someone who lost a pet if you've never had one? Or someone who had to work to put themselves through school if you were more fortunate financially? These situations require that you reflect on what your partner's "story" means to them, carefully observing their nonverbal cues and asking appropriate questions to more accurately interpret their words.

Activities to Develop Cognitive Empathy

Activity 1
Your life experiences form the basis of your assumptions and shape your expectations.

a) Make a special effort to interact with people you don't believe share your values and opinions, or who come from a background different from your own. Even in a classroom, your experiences, motivations, and priorities are probably not exactly the same as those of your fellow students.

b) Pair up with a partner who you don't know well. Select one of the topics below to discuss.

- How do you feel about gun control?
- Do you think everyone is entitled to healthcare, even if they can't afford it?
- Do you think family size should be limited?

c) Then, ask yourself the following questions. (This is a good exercise to follow, both in this conversation as well as in future communications.)

   1) Do I demonstrate a fundamental respect for my partner as we begin this conversation?
   2) Have I assessed my own nonverbal response and communicated warmth and openness?
   3) Am I sensitive to my partner's nonverbal cues?
   4) Have I heightened my awareness of my personal opinions, feelings, and attitudes so that they do not inhibit me from listening?
   5) Have I worked in other ways to create a supportive environment?

Activity 2
Think back and discuss the specific people who shaped your attitudes toward each of the following:

- healthcare
- education
- travel
- gender roles
- drugs
- the environment

a) What messages did they send?
b) Were they persuasive?
c) Do you still agree with their position?

Activity 3
Make a list of your five best friends.

a) In what ways are they similar to you? To each other?
b) In what ways are they different from you? From each other?
c) Are there any friends on the list with whom you have had trouble developing cognitive empathy? Explain why this might be the case.

Activity 4
In a group, identify a conflict situation or disagreement that could result from differences in perception due to the requirements of a particular role. Begin by focusing on the following role relationships:

1) student/teacher
2) parent/child
3) supervisor/administrative assistant

4) doctor/patient
5) husband/wife (or other partner/partner relationship)

a) Role play the conflict. Discuss how it might have been avoided had the perspectives of the other individual been taken more fully into consideration.
b) Role play the situation a second time, attempting to resolve the conflict through empathy and perspective-taking.
c) Did it work? Are there some conflicts that cannot be resolved in this manner? Elaborate.

Activity 5
In your group, discuss the importance of cognitive empathy in communication.

a) What can you do as a listener to foster and maintain open attitudes among diverse individuals?
b) What role does effective listening play in creating positive relationships? Provide concrete examples.

Activity 6
Describe awkward or frustrating situations group members have had visiting:

1) other families who are different from theirs in important ways (size, living arrangement, social environment, etc.)
2) other parts of the United States
3) other countries

a) What differences were most striking and problematic?
b) How did you adjust your behavior and communication in each situation?

Listening Outcome 12: Develop Your EQ and Social Sensitivity for Perceptive Empathy

How well-developed is your emotional intelligence, what we call "EQ"? EQ requires the ability to recognize and use nonverbal cues to supplement your understanding of what someone says. This ability is extremely important to many situations you will encounter where the other person is emotional. Improving your perceptive empathy—your ability to identify emotions that the communicator is experiencing—requires that you pay attention to a number of different cues. Your goal is to understand the person speaking, not just the meaning of his or her words. The richer the nonverbal dimension, the better able you will be to accurately interpret what you hear (see Box 6.1).

While speakers may occasionally manipulate these nonverbal elements, in most cases the information you obtain from nonverbal indicators more accurately reflects feelings than what the person says they are experiencing. Can you think of examples where that is the case?

BOX 6.1 RECOGNIZE NONVERBAL BEHAVIOR

Body Orientation and Posture

Receptiveness is communicated through an open, relaxed posture. A comfortable yet attentive pose lets others know that you are ready to listen and to help.

a) *Who do you know that makes you feel important by the way they listen nonverbally? What do they do?*

b) *Are you generally conscious of your nonverbal "attentive" behaviors? Do you think you send positive, professional messages through your posture and body orientation?*

Eye Contact

Eye contact lets others know that you are interested in what they have to say and that they have your full attention. The norms of eye behavior differ significantly from one culture to the next. Eye contact is one of the best ways for you to communicate empathy and understanding.

a) *Is eye contact comfortable for you, or do you have to work at maintaining it during a conversation?*

b) *Under what circumstances do you have the most trouble maintaining eye contact?*

Body Tension and Movement

Effective listeners are physically ready for an interaction; they look interested and alert. Random movements and fidgeting communicate impatience, boredom, or nervousness. Speakers may take those behaviors as a sign that you aren't concentrating or that you're anxious to be somewhere else.

a) *What mannerisms communicate boredom or impatience? How might they affect your conversations?*

b) *Do you have a particular nonverbal habit that you would like to break?*

Facial Expression

Your face conveys a range of emotions and has a significant effect on communication. It is important to be aware of what your face is communicating. You will appear more approachable if you demonstrate what we call a "positive affect," which means that your facial expressions are friendly and positive.

a) *Are you ever surprised when you look in the mirror and see your facial expression? What does your face generally convey?*
b) *Do your friends or others generally find you approachable?*

Minimal Reinforcers
As a listener you can demonstrate your understanding and interest through small behaviors such as nodding and even tilting your head to one side. Periodically say things like, "I see." Other short indicators are helpful as well. Minimal reinforcers encourage the speaker to continue. In some instances. silence is also an option.

a) *Do you think there are gender and cultural differences in the use of minimal reinforcers?*
b) *How comfortable are you with silence?*

Voice
Voice can be altered on the dimensions of rate, pitch, and volume. You can often tell a speaker's age, gender, mood, nationality, and other factors just from his or her voice. Judgments are made about things like personality, attitude, and level of interest from hearing someone speak. Voice is also a powerful tool in communicating emotional meaning.

a) *How would you describe your voice? Does it generate credibility?*
b) *Do you have a friend or family member who could benefit from speaking more loudly, or slowly?*

Skills for Success

1. Interpret Facial Expression and Eye Behavior
The face conveys a tremendous amount of information. In fact, every feature of your face changes with your emotional state, whether you are aware of it or not. When expressions are unintentional, it is called "leakage"; that is, your face is likely to express your true feelings, which you may not always want to share with your communication partner. By paying attention to facial expressions you will have a much better chance of accurately interpreting what you hear.

Perhaps eye contact is one of the most powerful indicators of effective listening. You can tell a great deal about someone by paying attention to his eyes, whether the person stares, looks away, or focuses on another activity.

While most of us assume that strong eye contact means that the person is listening, you realize that there is really no way of knowing for sure by nonverbal indicators alone. And, culturally, what is positive eye contact in one country may be rude or inappropriate in another.

2. Interpret Vocal Cues

What assumptions do you make just from hearing someone's voice? Age? Gender? Intelligence? Nationality? Emotional state? Voice provides numerous clues that either reinforce or contradict the verbal message. Key features of voice include rate (fast/slow), volume (loud/soft), and pitch (high/low). As you can probably guess, when someone is angry her voice is likely to become faster, louder, and higher. Sadness is usually conveyed by a softer volume and slower pace. You may hear voice described as "cracking," "raspy," or "breathy." These qualities, along with the other dimensions, contribute to your perceptions and help you accurately interpret the speaker's message.

3. Listen to Interpret Mediated Communication

Mediated communication is carried out through the use of some form of technology. Listening to mediated communication is particularly challenging because you often have fewer nonverbal indicators to shape your interpretation of the message. Online you may have just text, or text and perhaps graphics. When you communicate through Skype or Zoom, you may feel you are "connected," but there is still a perceptual distance that impacts your behavior and response in ways that make understanding more difficult and more uncertain. What to do? First, be selective about when you agree to communication at a distance. Always check your perceptions to make sure that you have accurately understood the intended message.

4. Interpret Appearance

An individual's overall appearance also influences your perceptions and interpretation of the messages you receive. While it is important to acknowledge this nonverbal element, once again it is important to be aware of your own mental framework and potential bias. You might intentionally—or unintentionally—assign meanings to features that may not be valid indicators. Someone is dressed poorly—what does that mean? Someone is bundled up on a hot day—you ask yourself why. We seem to readily assign more credibility to speakers who are well-dressed, poised, and appear confident. Yet, these nonverbal cues may or may not correlate with the judgments we've made.

Activities to Develop Social Sensitivity and Perceptive Empathy

Activity 1

Make a habit of observing people in various communication situations. Consider the impact of their nonverbal behavior on their relationships.

a)   Identify three people you would describe as "highly effective listeners." Observe at least one of them "in action" as they communicate.

    a)   What nonverbal behaviors did you notice?

    b)   What earned them the description of "highly effective listener"?

    c)   If someone from another culture was asked this question, would she draw the same conclusion about the person's listening effectiveness?

Activity 2

Observe a conversation in which you are not participating but which is occurring close enough that you can hear everything that is said.

    As you watch, do the following.

a)   Describe the nonverbal behaviors you notice.

b)   Determine whether the nonverbal behaviors are intentional or unintentional.

c)   Identify the emotions that are being communicated through facial expressions.

d)   Explain how body posture and movement provide cues to emotional states.

e)   Notice any silences—what might they communicate?

f)   If you don't know the communicators, can you make a guess as to their relationship?

Activity 3

Think about the extent to which social sensitivity comes naturally and the extent to which you make a conscious effort to develop or increase this awareness.

a)   How do people differ in perceptive empathy?

b)   What might you do to enhance this ability? Do you agree that you can increase your EQ through focused efforts? Is it a communication competence everyone can learn or develop?

c)   How do members of your family differ with regard to perceptive empathy? Give examples.

Activity 4

Voice plays a key role in communicating emotions.

a)   Take turns reading the following sentences and phrases. In each case, the speaker selects an emotion and attempts to convey it to other members of the group through vocal characteristics.

- I thought so.
- Not if I can help it.

- I love that car.
- Can't wait to see her.
- Go ahead, bring it closer.
- Take your time.
- That takes care of it.
  Sample emotions: Sad, angry, reluctant, happy, upset, sarcastic, fearful, disgusted, surprised.

b) Guess the emotion; see how accurately you can identify the emotion that is being expressed.
c) Did different group members perceive different emotions? Why might that be the case?

Activity 5
Determine how much information you derive from someone's appearance, and whether or not the stereotypes you may be using and the assumptions you make are accurate.

a) How do clothes, for instance, influence your perceptions? Begin by taking a close look in your own closet. What generalizations can you make about the clothes you've chosen? How would you describe your wardrobe?
b) Do you think that your assumptions help you listen more effectively, or do they interfere with your ability to make accurate judgments? Explain.
c) Think about the nonverbal indicators you use to make judgments about an individual you don't know well. Then, provide two adjectives that reveal your assumptions about each of the following individuals based on stereotypes regarding their appearance.

1) An older woman dressed in a short skirt and revealing top.
2) A young man with tattoos covering his body.
3) A child in a uniform.
4) A young woman in ill-fitting, dirty clothes.
5) A middle-aged man in an expensive suit and conservative tie.
6) A teenager with numerous piercings smoking a cigarette.

Listening Outcome 13: Demonstrate Behavioral Empathy

You want others to know that you care about them and that you are working to understand their experiences and their feelings. It's clear that your client or friend may be having a difficult time sharing their thoughts and you want to encourage them to continue. One powerful way to communicate your acceptance and understanding is through a verbal and nonverbal response that demonstrates your concern. When you project a genuine interest in someone and

---

BOX 6.2 WARM VERSUS COLD NONVERBAL BEHAVIORS

Warm Behaviors—Approachable	Cold Behaviors—"Leave Me Alone"
Maintaining direct eye contact	Staring
Smiling	Looking away
Nodding head	Shaking head negatively
Leaning forward	Nervous habits, fidgeting
Maintaining a positive facial expression	Maintaining a negative facial expression
Using minimal reinforcers	Being unresponsive

---

an openness to hear what they have to say—largely through nonverbal cues—you're practicing behavioral empathy.

The problem is that it's often difficult to know exactly how you're coming across to another person. You may think that you are receptive and positive, but your nonverbal behaviors may reflect something different (Box 6.2). If someone was to hold up a mirror in front of you as you walked across campus, sat in a classroom, or listened to a friend's conversation, would you know what emotions they would think you were experiencing? Do you look approachable, or disagreeable? Heightening your awareness of your own nonverbal response is the first step in demonstrating the behavioral empathy needed to be perceived as a supportive listener.

Skills for Success

1. Personal Factors Affect Perceptions of Empathy
Your ability to empathize varies with your attitude, personality, and motivation. Perhaps one of the most essential personal characteristics for behavioral empathy is warmth. There are a number of specific nonverbal behaviors associated with openness and caring, and it is useful to do a self-assessment to determine whether there are any nonverbal behaviors that you might want to strengthen.

2. Respond in an Accepting, Non-judgmental Manner
When someone tells you about a problem your typical response—perhaps it's humor or disbelief—may not always be the most effective. This is especially true if your goal is to project empathy and support (Box 6.3). Since it is always difficult to see ourselves objectively, you might ask a trusted friend to provide some constructive feedback on how readily and clearly you project your interest and concern. Remember, too, that your communication partner

---

BOX 6.3 BENEFITS OF DEMONSTRATING EMPATHY

- Increases trust and respect
- Enables others to express emotions productively
- Reduces tensions
- Encourages the surfacing of information that may have been difficult to communicate
- Creates a safe environment for sharing and problem-solving
- Builds the other person's confidence

---

is responding to the way you behave; if you want to strengthen your relationship and demonstrate that your compassion is genuine, pay close attention to your nonverbal cues so that you are viewed as empathic and engaged.

3. Provide Minimal Reinforcers
Sometimes you can have the most positive effect on a relationship and communicate behavioral empathy simply by providing what we call minimal reinforcers—a nod, "I see," or "Yes," "Go on," "Right."

These cues demonstrate your continuing interest and involvement without taking the focus away from the speaker. Often, listeners think that they are being empathic by interrupting with their own stories or experiences that relate to the speaker's topic or situation. However, this response takes the focus away from your partner and places it on you. Let the speaker continue uninterrupted, even if she pauses or hesitates. Be patient.

4. Use a Paraphrase to Reflect Both Content and Feelings
You've likely heard the term "paraphrase." In the context of listening, it means that you absorb another person's thoughts *and feelings* and then, in your own words, repeat the central message so that your partner knows you understood what was said. This simple activity forces you to focus on the content of the message and to concentrate on understanding not only the words, but also what the speaker is feeling. It is helpful to the speaker because it allows them to reflect on their message and clarify their thoughts. Paraphrasing is similar to perception-checking but encompasses an additional component, the emotional message. It is also done to be helpful to the speaker rather than serving to clarify information for the listener's benefit.

5. Consider Proxemics
Imagine that a friend yells from across the parking lot, "How was that hot date with Jamie last night?!" What would you say? For most of us, it would seem awkward to shout back personal details of our night out—the friend is just too

far away to carry on a personal conversation. Proxemics, or the distance between communicators, influences your comfort level when you share information. There may be times you're too far away, and other times when the speaker is so close that you become distracted and can't listen. Think back about your listening experiences and see if you can identify an occasion where the other person was just... in your face! Each of us has a "personal bubble" that surrounds us. If it is invaded, we become stressed and anxious, making it nearly impossible to listen effectively. On the other hand, if you are in a lounge where seating is spaced too far apart, conversation can also be negatively affected due to the fact that you have to speak so loudly to be heard. It's up to you, then, to make sure your partner or group members are at a distance that makes effective listening possible.

Activities to Develop Behavioral Empathy

Activity 1
Notice how much eye contact you use in your daily interactions.

a) Under what circumstances is your eye contact strong—who are you listening to or talking with when you feel most comfortable maintaining eye contact?
b) In what situations do you have trouble maintaining your focus on the other person?
c) Do you find it easiest to maintain eye contact when you are speaking or listening?
d) Do you have the strongest eye contact with your classmates or your professor? With your parents or with your friends? Think of other comparisons and reflect on what these differences mean for the effectiveness of your listening.

Activity 2
How did you learn appropriate eye behavior?

a) In your group, brainstorm the ways that you use eye contact and identify the "norms" of eye behavior in the United States.
b) See if anyone in your class is an international student or has lived in another country. If so, ask them to discuss eye behavior in that environment.
c) Look up information on eye behavior in at least two foreign countries and compare it to the United States.

Activity 3
In a group, generate a list of eye behavior norms for the United States.

a) Ask each member of your group to identify a norm that they will break within the next several days. For instance, you might stare at someone in an elevator, look intently at your partner's elbow as you speak, etc.
b) After seeking out these opportunities, regroup to discuss what happened.

   1) Was breaking a norm difficult for you?
   2) What was the other person's response?
   3) How does breaking a norm affect your communication? How about your listening?

Activity 4
See if you can master the skill of paraphrasing by reflecting both the speaker's content and her feelings, as expressed in the following sentences. Take turns reading each of the sentences aloud to your classmates and, after each reading, ask someone in your group to paraphrase. Be sure to speak up if you disagree with your classmates' interpretations.

1) Hey, leave that alone! It's mine!
2) Why don't you just tell me what's wrong? All you do is mope around, feeling sorry for yourself.
3) No wonder he got the promotion over me. He's been kissing up to our supervisor for a year—it's disgusting.
4) Hey, you won't believe this! I just won the door prize of a new laptop!
5) Too many things are going wrong. I feel like a witch cast some sort of spell on me.
6) She's never satisfied, no matter what I do. I might as well just stop trying to please.

Activity 5
Sometimes you're required to express emotions that you don't really feel. This is called "emotional labor."

a) Describe an experience you've had that required emotional labor. Perhaps it was a customer service job, a wedding, or an interview.
b) How easily can you project expected feelings that might not be completely authentic?
c) What did you learn about yourself from this experience?
d) Do you know someone who is particularly good at projecting emotions they don't genuinely feel? What are the possible negative implications or impact of this behavior—both for the individual and for effective communication?

Activity 6
While you discussed how others' appearance affects perceptive empathy, it is also helpful to think about your personal choices that influence how comfortable a speaker is communicating with you.

a)   How do you think a friend would describe you based on your appearance? How about someone who passes you on the street or sees you on campus dining?
b)   Have you ever had an interview where someone evaluated you based on how you looked? What were your strengths in that situation?
c)   Do you believe there are ethical concerns when important decisions are made on the basis of someone's appearance?
d)   Some organizations use appearance as a criterion when they interview and hire employees. What are the advantages and disadvantages of this practice?

Activity 7
Touch also affects listening effectiveness. It can bring people closer together or cause discomfort.

a)   How does touch affect perceptions of listening?
b)   What influences your comfort with physical contact—are you more likely to touch some individuals than others? What variables do you consider?
c)   What were you taught about touching behavior as you were growing up? Do you believe that these "guidelines" are still appropriate?
d)   How is touching perceived differently in different cultures?
e)   How does touching affect your listening?

Activity 8
The physical distance between communicators has a significant impact on their speaking and listening.
    Find a partner among your classmates and stand face-to-face at a distance of about seven feet. Begin a casual conversation. As you talk, slowly begin moving closer together until one of you stops the conversation to say, "Okay! This is close enough!"

a)   Do you think you get closer or farther away from your communication partner than most other people your age?
b)   What variables affect your comfort level and "social distance" in this situation?
c)   What behaviors do people exhibit when they begin to feel the other person is getting too close?
d)   How does your unique relationship affect your listening behavior?

Assess Your Current Listening Behavior: Interpreting

Rate your *interpreting* on the following scale of 1 to 5.

_____5. Everyone thinks that I am extremely good at "reading" people. I notice their nonverbal communication and, no surprise, I am very expressive myself. I let others know that I am listening to them through my facial expressions, eye contact, and other cues. I am very aware of the impression I make.

_____4. I've always thought of myself as someone who was socially sensitive; that is, I quickly notice if someone seems upset or angry or anxious by observing their nonverbal behaviors. When someone else is speaking I think I'm a responsive listener, providing nonverbal cues that let them know I'm listening.

_____3. Nonverbal communication is important—it usually gives me reliable information about how someone feels about what's going on. I try to pay attention to it and not get carried away, and I also think I am fairly expressive myself.—in a good way.

_____2. Nonverbal behavior helps with communication, I don't doubt that, but I usually pay more attention to what someone says. Sometimes I'm not even looking at them, so I really can't use nonverbal cues. I don't know about my own nonverbal behavior. I guess it's okay.

_____1. I've always been a little suspicious about "reading" nonverbal behavior. What if I get it wrong? So, I really don't think much about it one way or the other.

7

LISTEN TO EVALUATE

Outcomes

When you're bombarded with messages everywhere you go, whether they reach you online or in person, it's important to have some way of judging the validity and reliability of what you hear. When you evaluate messages, you ask yourself questions that enable you to determine whether what someone says is a fact or an assumption, whether they are biased or objective, credible or a jerk. Credibility is an often-neglected dimension of listening that has to do with the speaker's expertise and trustworthiness. In that regard, effective listeners learn to identify those messages that rely almost exclusively on emotional appeals and propaganda devices for their impact. It is also important to view incoming information with an ethical lens to ensure that the decisions you make bring no harm to others.

Listening Outcome E1: Analyze Speaker Credibility

"Who is this person, anyway? How do I determine if he knows what he's talking about?" If you don't trust the accuracy of what you hear, it may be because there are some speakers who just don't seem credible.

Trust is a fascinating concept. Think of the people you find trustworthy and ask yourself what factors contribute to your perceptions. Generally, trust is developed over time as you discover that you can depend on what a person says—that they are competent and honest. Credible individuals are also perceived as fair-minded and proactive. They have what we call a "positive affect"; they look at what is possible and inspire their friends and colleagues to do the same.

Credibility also has to do with perceptions of the speaker's character. While you may not know the person before he speaks, you form an impression of his trustworthiness during the communication encounter itself. This suggests that whether you know the person or not when he begins (initial credibility), credibility can be derived during the speech or conversation so that by the time he is finished talking (terminal credibility), you have a strong sense of whether or not you should believe his message.

Skills for Success

1. Consider the Speaker's Reputation and Expertise
Some speakers just seem credible. They are poised, polished, and you quickly believe what they have to say. Because your first impression can be misleading, it's good to step back and ask yourself whether the person is in a position to really know about the topic. What is his or her experience? What are his motives? Do you have any reason not to trust what he tells you about this subject? When you're listening to someone, it's always helpful to find out as much about them as you can.

2. Distinguish Among Initial, Derived, and Terminal Credibility
While it's important to establish the speaker's credibility from the onset, you may have a different impression once the person begins speaking. Credibility that is established due to the specific communication is called "derived." As the speaker talks, you make your own independent judgment regarding his trustworthiness and expertise so that, when he finishes, his terminal credibility may be somewhat different—either higher or lower—than when he began.

Activities to Assess Speaker Credibility

Activity 1
Analyze your personal credibility by discussing the following questions.

a) On what topics do you have credibility? How was it developed? Are you sure you have it with everyone?
b) On what subjects is your credibility low? Do you ever find yourself talking about subjects in which you have almost no credibility? What is the experience like?
c) On what topics would you like to increase your credibility? What could you do to make this happen?

Activity 2
Rank order the following occupations according to the *importance of credibility* to each profession (1 = least need for credibility, 10 = most need). Now rate

	Importance of Credibility	Perceptions of Credibility
1) college teacher	____	____
2) surgeon	____	____
3) pilot	____	____
4) truck driver	____	____
5) home contractor	____	____
6) car salesperson	____	____
7) cruise ship captain	____	____
8) tradesperson	____	____
9) artist	____	____

them again according to which you believe to be most credible in the United States.

a) Compare your responses to those of your classmates.
b) Discuss the reasons for your ranking, and why there might be differences.
c) Do you think there are cultural differences in the occupations perceived as most credible?

Activity 3
With your group members, generate a list of pubic personalities—from movies, politics, or sports—whom you respect. Create a second list of those you distrust.

a) What did each person do to influence your perceptions of his or her credibility?
b) How do your perceptions of credibility influence the way you listen?
c) Do you agree more frequently with people whom you perceive as credible?
d) Try to determine the origin of any perceptual differences among members of your group. How do an individual's interests and background affect judgments of credibility?

Activity 4
Think of an example of someone who you thought wasn't credible but who was able to increase his or her credibility as you listened to them speak, or as you got to know them better through your communications. What did they do to change your perception?

Listening Outcome E2: Determine the Ethical Dimensions of the Situation

As a listener, you are constantly bombarded with messages. In many cases, the ideas you hear are meant to influence or persuade you to take action or to adopt a specific point of view. When you do make a decision, you're probably taking many things into consideration. Some of this happens as the result of a deliberate effort, but other factors in your decision-making process occur almost automatically. Different listeners have different priorities and this influences the basis used for making choices.

One decision-making lens that is often overlooked is ethics. While you may ask yourself questions like "Does it make money?" or "How hard would it be to do?" many listeners are much less likely to ask "Is this ethical—is it the 'right' thing to do?" If you listen closely, you'll discover that there's almost always an ethical dimension to messages. Unless you deliberately focus on the ethical aspects, however, it's easy to overlook. What you say is a direct reflection of who you are; your response conveys your character and integrity. It's important to distinguish the difference between those messages that are ethical and those that may be self-serving or ignore the potential of negative impacts on others.

Skills for Success

1. Examine the Message with an Ethical Lens
Whenever you have a difficult decision to make, there are a number of criteria that probably come to mind immediately. It often takes a deliberate effort, however, to ensure that your decision is also ethical. The more significant the decision is—the greater the number of people affected—the more important it is to stop and reflect on whether it is the "right" thing to

---

BOX 7.1 STEPHEN HALL'S SEVEN TESTS FOR ETHICAL DECISION-MAKING

1. Is what I am deciding legal?
2. Will my decision hurt anyone?
3. Is my decision fair to all?
4. Am I being honest?
5. Can I live with my decision?
6. Would I be willing to publicly announce my decision?
7. What if everyone did what I am about to do?

do. An ethicist, Stephen Hall, developed a set of questions that you can ask to determine if the decision you are about to make has ethical dimensions (see Box 7.1).

2. Determine if there is More to Know about the Person and Situation
There may be occasions when you listen to someone and think, "That doesn't sound ethical to me." In such situations, you are likely to make a quick assessment that the person is unethical and perhaps manipulative or purposefully deceitful. Rather than drawing hasty conclusions, think about the person's past experiences, background, and culture. Often, ethical standards vary and it may be that what you question as unethical is perfectly acceptable given the background of the person speaking. What happens then is up to you.

3. Reaffirm Your Own Values and Know Your Organization's Ethical Code
Often an individual's behavior, and what they consider acceptable, is influenced by the standards set by their organizations. Each organization has its own ethical culture and, before joining a company, it is helpful to find out more about its expectations. Regardless of how much you might like a particular job, sooner or later you will be confronted with difficult ethical decisions. You will want to know that you're a member of an organization with a strong sense of fairness and social responsibility.

Your values influence almost every decision you make and serve as the basis for how you choose your friends, establish your priorities, and decide on a career. It's important, then, to be clear about what you believe—what you think is right, good, or fair under various circumstances. Only when you know where you stand on important value issues will you be able to critically listen to others.

Activities to Determine the Ethical Dimensions of a Situation

Activity 1
Do you believe that, as a listener, you share the speaker's ethical responsibility? That is, when you hear something you believe is unethical, should you speak up?

a)   With your classmates, discuss your thoughts on the scope of your personal responsibility to reveal unethical practices or publicly question unethical positions.
b)   Do the specific circumstances make a difference?
c)   Describe an ethical issue that you, or someone you know, has heard and then confronted. What was the outcome?

Activity 2
Discuss the following questions with members of your class.

a) Does your school or organization have an ethical code?
b) Does everyone know about it?
c) Do you believe it encourages individuals to behave more ethically and responsibly?
d) Is there something that could be done so that it better serves its purpose?

Activity 3
Identify a recent event that has generated an ethical dilemma. You can get ideas from the internet or other sources.

a) What are the various sides of the issue?
b) As a listener, what position do you take on the issue?
c) Does the medium matter—in other words, does something seem more or less ethical when it is received through a website or blog?
d) Would you describe yourself as "ethically sensitive"? That is, do you quickly recognize ethical dilemmas when they arise?

Activity 4
As you may know, ethical frameworks differ according to cultural norms. Is there any way, then, that an ethical culture can be created when working in a multicultural environment? Discuss the potential issues with your classmates. Generate a list of recommendations for creating an ethical culture when an organization is extremely diverse.

Activity 5
One of the most useful tools in determining whether a behavior is ethical is to apply Hall's Seven Questions to the situation.

a) Read the following scenarios and then, in a small group, discuss each of Hall's Seven Questions to determine whether the behavior is ethical.
b) The next time you confront an ethical dilemma, see if this framework helps you make a mindful and ethical decision.

Scenario
You work in a hotel. You learn that your married co-worker, the Lounge Manager, is having an affair with one of the bartenders, who reports to her. The Lounge Manager is a close, personal friend and your families are also quite close. You can tell that their relationship is having a disruptive influence on her work.

Is her behavior ethical?
What should you do?

Scenario

You're a manager in a company that is being downsized and you have privileged information regarding a number of employees who will be losing their jobs. You discover that one of these employees, a single mother of three, is planning to make a purchase that will stretch her existing limited income and will clearly create a hardship when she loses her job. You know that there are no exceptions to the company's policy of making all announcements at a predetermined time and not before, but you'd really like to prevent her from making a big mistake.

Would telling her about the downsizing be ethical?
What should you do?

Listening Outcome E3: Analyze Evidence and Reasoning

Speakers who are fluent and confident often give the impression that they know what they're talking about—when maybe they don't. It's your responsibility as a listener to assess the arguments you hear and test the evidence and reasoning to be sure that you are supporting someone who has been responsible in her presentation and sound in her thinking. By following a few guidelines, you will be able to analyze the speaker's selection and use of information (Box 7.2). When speakers feel strongly about their message it's easy for them to justify persuasive tactics that may be effective but that aren't accurate, representative, or logical.

Skills for Success

1. Distinguish Facts from Inferences and Opinions

When evaluating what you hear, a first step is to determine whether the information is factual—something that can be verified—or whether it's the speaker's opinion. If it's a matter of fact, you can stop arguing, since everyone

---

BOX 7.2 TASKS FOR THE CRITICAL LISTENER

- Judge the validity and adequacy of arguments.
- Distinguish facts from opinions and inferences.
- Identify logical fallacies.
- Identify propaganda appeals.
- Detect speaker bias.
- Determine speaker credibility.

should be able to agree. "It's 12 miles to the nearest restaurant"; "24 students went on the field trip." Sometimes facts are unknown and assumptions are made. Sooner or later, however, a fact can be verified and will provide the most reliable evidence.

When logic is required, it is also important to identify inferences. Inferences cannot be obtained by direct observation but, rather, are "good guesses." When you make an inference, you are jumping from observable facts to a likely or probable outcome. Often, inferences are the result of the speaker adding information to what is already known so that a decision can be made and action taken.

Similarly, opinions are often unique to the communicator and are based on a combination of facts, assumptions, and other personal motivations. Opinions, unlike facts, can be modified and changed. What one person thinks is "best," another may try to avoid. When you disagree with someone and hold a different opinion, it may be because you are looking at a different set of facts or different dimensions of a problem. Or perhaps your goals are different and you therefore believe in different strategies or want different outcomes. We said it was 12 miles to the nearest restaurant. Is that a "long way"? Or perhaps it's "a short drive"? Regardless of the situation, it is important for you to identify opinions and distinguish them from the facts that everyone can agree on (Box 7.3).

BOX 7.3 ANALYZE EVIDENCE AND REASONING

Determine whether what you hear is a fact, inference, or opinion.

Fact—can be made only after direct observation

Inference—goes beyond what was observed into interpretation; presented in terms of probability

Opinion—interpreted personally in light of individual values and bias

Determine whether the speaker is credible.

Are all or most references to personal experiences?

Does he cite reliable sources?

Is the delivery effective and powerful?

Does the speaker seem to understand his listeners' needs?

Does the speaker create rapport with his listeners?

Determine whether the evidence used is sound.

Statistics—how were they gathered? Are they sufficient? Representative?

Testimony—is it directly related to the point? Is it recent? Is the source reliable?

Comparisons—are the things being compared similar in important ways?

Examples—are they relevant? Are there exceptions that should be considered?

2. Identify Types of Evidence and Support
How much evidence does it take to convince you that the bus is too unreliable to use? Or that you should see a doctor about your sore throat? The answer is, "it depends." There are a number of different types of evidence and each affects you in different ways. Perhaps the easiest evidence to identify is statistics, which help to make assertions specific and concrete. Just numbers, however, can be misleading. It is important to ask yourself related questions, such as the following.

a) How were the numbers gathered?
b) Are they recent and were they obtained in a reliable manner?
c) Can the results be verified in other ways—do they make sense?

In addition to statistics, evidence may be also be provided in several other ways, such as in the form of testimony or stories. Again, it is important to make sure your source is credible and free from bias.

Activities to Effectively Analyze Evidence and Reasoning

Activity 1
Let's make this activity all about you as a listener and reflect on the following questions.

a) What inferences have others made about you? On what basis was the inference made? Was it true?
b) What can you learn about yourself from the things others assume are true about you?
c) What do you do when false information is circulated?

Activity 2
Along with a group of your classmates, prepare in writing a set of instructions for someone to put on a coat. Assume the "actor" knows nothing about coats —he would not understand terms like collar, lapel, lining, belt, pocket, buttons, and so forth.

a) Read your directions to an individual who was not a member of your group. Ask him to follow your directions exactly as you read them. For instance, you might start by saying, "Pick up the piece of blue material on the chair..."
b) The individual who is reading should have her back to the "actor." The speaker cannot add any information to what was written down, and the "actor" can do only what he is instructed to do without asking any questions.
c) After the exercise, discuss the following questions.

1) Were the directions complete?
2) Did the "actor" end up wearing the coat?
3) What assumptions were made?

d) Using the same instructions as above, read the directions again to another "actor," this time allowing for questions and perception-checking.
e) How do the two attempts compare? Did the ability to ask questions make a difference?

Activity 3
Review the list of statements below and determine what it would take to convince you to accept the position being advocated. In other words, how much, and what type, of "evidence" would you need to be persuaded? Write down your response.

• Spain is the most beautiful European country.
• Gun control does not prevent or reduce violence.
• A college degree is not worth the money.
• Married men are happier than bachelors.
• A middle child has less self-esteem than an eldest child.
• Cruises are the best way to see the world.

Now, take turns sharing your response with the rest of the class or with other group members.

a) Are there differences in the type and amount of "evidence" individuals would require?
b) What accounts for these differences?
c) If someone wants to be persuasive, how does she know what evidence to provide?

Activity 4

a) Select one of the topics listed below.

Topic	Listener(s)
Join our Zumba class	working mothers
Don't wait to plan for retirement	sales personnel
A kitten makes the best pet	kindergarten class
Recycle	lawyers
The ends justify the means	college students

b)   In your group, discuss how you would adapt your message for each set of listeners by selecting the most relevant and appropriate evidence to support your point.

c)   Note how you might adapt other features of the message—language, length, and so forth—to be most effective with a particular listener.

Activity 5

Keep a personal journal and record disagreements or arguments you have with friends or family members. There may be some individuals with whom you disagree more frequently than others.

Select one specific, note-worthy example of a conflict and respond to the following questions.

a)   How rational were you? How about your communication partner?

b)   Did you get the feeling that the other person was listening to you?

c)   What was the outcome of the disagreement? Do disagreements with this person end in the same way most of the time?

d)   What behaviors would be more productive—what can you do to facilitate effective listening on both sides?

Listening Outcome E4: Identify Emotional Appeals

Although we know that listening effectiveness decreases when you become emotional, persuasive appeals that connect with emotions can be very powerful. In fact, there are many situations where logic alone cannot change someone's mind or convince someone to act. In such cases, communicators rely on an emotional response to achieve their desired results, whether it be persuading teenagers to wear seat belts or children to brush their teeth. While in most cases an emotional appeal is harmless and effective, there may be some occasions when the speaker takes advantage of listeners who don't recognize that they are being influenced in the absence of evidence and logic. Effective listeners analyze the messages they hear to become more aware of the types of appeals being used.

Skills for Success

1. Recognize Values

To really understand another person, you need to identify her values. It's easy to make the assumption that you and your communication partner are more similar than you actually are unless you listen closely. Ask yourself, "What is important to my client or friend?" The language she uses, the examples she provides, the priorities she sets, the emphasis she places on certain components of the message—all of these things personalize her communication. The only way to really identify someone else's values is if you listen actively and focus your full attention on the speaker with this purpose in mind.

2. Identify Propaganda Techniques
Name-calling, card-stacking, the bandwagon, glittering generality, doublespeak —all are examples of common propaganda techniques that speakers use to influence and persuade. Box 7.4 briefly describes each technique. You won't

---

BOX 7.4 PROPAGANDA TECHNIQUES

The skilled critical listener identifies, and discounts, propaganda techniques such as the following.

1. *Name-calling.* In name-calling, the speaker gives a person or an idea a negative label without providing any evidence to prove the assertion. When you hear a speaker call someone a "liar," "crook," or "jerk," don't be misled. Make sure the speaker presents good reasons for using these emotion-laden labels.
2. *Card-stacking.* Card-stacking is a method in which the speaker, instead of presenting all of the important evidence, tells you only those facts that support the point she is trying to make. The communicator leaves out the negative aspect of the idea and neglects to point out any benefits of other positions.
3. *The bandwagon.* In this appeal, the speaker tries to convince you to "jump on the bandwagon" by telling you that everyone else is doing something—whether it is purchasing a computer or drinking a certain beverage. The implication is that you should do it, too, or you will be left out.
4. *Glittering generality.* A glittering generality is a word so vague that everyone agrees on its appropriateness and value—but no one is really sure just what it means. If your instructor says she is in favor of "fair grading policies" or "flexibility in the submission of assignments," she is using a glittering generality.
5. *Testimonial.* When a communicator presents the opinion of some well-known person to support his view, the strategy is called a *testimonial.* Often, the particular individual, although famous, is not qualified to judge or speak on the idea he advocates.
6. *Doublespeak.* When you hear that a communicator is using doublespeak, it means that she is trying *not* to communicate clearly and accurately. It is likely that she is concealing the truth and deliberately misleading or distracting you.

have any trouble finding examples in the media, online, and in your everyday communication with friends and classmates because, unfortunately, propaganda is all too common. By developing your critical listening skills you will be able to avoid falling into the traps set by speakers who are hoping to influence you through devious or disingenuous means.

3. Recognize the Impact of Language

Language itself can have a significant impact and can create an emotional response. Think of your response to "help," "fire," "stop," or even swear words. Name-calling, as you know, can have a powerful emotional impact—especially when the label is discriminatory or disrespectful. There are times when speakers use "strategic ambiguity," language so vague that almost everyone can agree with their point. On other occasions, precision in language is critical to accomplish a purpose. Keep in mind, however, that words mean different things to different people depending on the context and their personal experiences, values, and background. If you've been bitten by a dog then the word "dog" is going to elicit a different response than someone who works as a vet or who uses a guide dog for assistance.

Activities to Identify Emotional Appeals

Activity 1

Go online and search for political messages that rely on propaganda techniques. Try to identify the specific techniques that were used in each. Bring three examples into class to discuss.

a)   Is the message effective?
b)   Can you profile the listener who would be most likely to be influenced by this message?
c)   What can the public do to protect itself from propaganda? Is it inevitable that politicians will use these devices?
d)   What do effective listeners need to know to avoid being deceived by propaganda strategies?

Activity 2

Emotional responses can be very powerful. As a listener, it's important to recognize them in all of your communications.

a)   Are you more likely to respond emotionally to a verbal or a written message? To a picture or to words?
b)   What types of emotional appeal affect you the most?
c)   Under what circumstances are you most likely to respond emotionally to a message?

Activity 3
Persuasive messages are likely to connect with values that are important to you —things like family, money, health, or popularity.

a)   What three values would you say are particularly important to you?
b)   Do you share any of these values with other members of your family? With your friends?
c)   What can you do to make sure that you continue to analyze a persuasive appeal even when it elicits a strong emotional response—and connects to a value you hold as a high priority?

Activity 4
Bring in a short passage that you believe will elicit a strong emotional response from members of a particular demographic. Read it to your group and then discuss the following.

a)   What type of listener is this message designed to persuade? Identify their most probable age, education level, gender, nationality, and so forth.
b)   What are the needs and values of the target group?
c)   How effective was the message in accomplishing its goal?
d)   How else might the author have persuaded this group?

Activity 5

a)   Select any multifaceted or unique product. You can use one of the products listed below or select another that you think would be interesting. Write down five to eight features of the product.
b)   Identify the specific characteristics of your intended market/listeners. Examples of "markets" are listed below, but there are many others you could use.
c)   In your group, create your own advertisement using appeals from the list of propaganda techniques below. It should have both pictures and text.
d)   Explain why this market is likely to be influenced by your appeals.

Propaganda Technique	*Product*	*Market—Characteristics*
1) The bandwagon	Drone	Teenagers
2) Card-Stacking	Tires	Older adults
3) Testimonial	Eye glasses	Children
4) Glittering generality	Sound system	Sports enthusiasts

Activity 6

Discuss the following questions with your classmates.

a)   Is logic valued more in some environments or situations than others?

b)   Do you believe there are gender differences in the degree to which decisions are made on an emotional basis? Cultural differences? Age differences?

c)   Under what circumstances do you believe it would be inappropriate to try to elicit an emotional response?

Listening Outcome E5: Listen Objectively

When someone disagrees with you, it's tempting to seek opportunities to refute the arguments you hear and to focus on making sure that you present your case in a compelling manner. Your immediate goal is to "win" the argument. But wait—listeners need to *listen*. Listening entails holding judgment and actually considering the possibility that your mind will be changed by the speaker's points. Instead of worrying about making your case, think about what you could learn from the other person. This requires adopting a new mental framework.

Skills for Success

1. Recognize that there's Always More to Know

Keep in mind that your point of view is based on what you know at the time. Even if you know a lot, you don't know everything. You can benefit most, then, by trying to learn as much as possible about the topic. Focusing on what someone with an opposing view has to say is a good first step. We tend to surround ourselves with ideas that confirm our position, so it takes a significant amount of effort to broaden our perspective and seek out new ideas and alternative viewpoints.

2. Focus on Individuals, Not on Categories

Another potentially harmful thought pattern is the tendency to use categories to determine characteristics about an individual. Similar to stereotyping, this type of thinking influences your expectations and subsequently your perceptions. It's difficult not to pre-judge when you have had previous experiences with "renters," or the "police," or "sales people." Just because you had a couple of renters who didn't take very good care of your apartment, however, doesn't mean that everyone who rents is unreliable. Overcoming this tendency is difficult, but a technique called "indexing" can be helpful. It asks you to focus on the characteristics of a single instance or individual rather than be influenced by the convenience of using categories to shape your judgments.

3. Things Can be Gray, Not Just Black and White

We're bombarded with so much information that it is often difficult to thoroughly and thoughtfully assess what we hear. It is much easier to simply accept what we agree with and disregard anything that doesn't readily fit our personal beliefs. Even language itself tends to push us to extremes—you can probably recall instances where your friends complained that a class was a "huge waste of time" or that the exam was "totally unfair." Keep in mind that, even when the amount of information you are confronted with seems overwhelming, it is important to clarify what you hear and to recognize that not everything fits neatly into "important" or "unimportant," "good" or "bad," "all black" or "all white."

4. Keep Emotions in Check

Recall that to listen well, you need to remain objective and open to a variety of viewpoints. While it may seem nearly impossible to keep your emotions in check, there are several techniques you can try. Recognize your triggers, the topics or people who elicit a strong emotional response (Box 7.5). Sometimes listeners have what we call semantic reactions. When this happens, your response is disproportionately strong given the stimulus. A good solution? Go away and come back later! If you are too emotionally involved or distracted to have an objective, reasonable conversation, then reschedule.

Activities to Facilitate Objective Listening

Activity 1

It's helpful to identify your strong opinions because they often lead to biases you didn't realize you had.

BOX 7.5 REDUCE THE IMPACT OF EMOTIONAL APPEALS

- Identify and acknowledge your "hot buttons," words or statements that immediately elicit an emotional response, such as, "it's not my job," or "sucker."
- Plan an "exit strategy" in advance for when you know you will become emotional in a situation. You know that if you continue, things will just get worse.
- Use self-talk to calm yourself and stay as objective as possible; take a deep breath, put things into perspective.
- Delay the conversation until you can think straight; arrange to come back, to get together at a later time.

---

a) List three of your very strong opinions—positions that you don't think can be changed through any additional information or argument.
b) Then, describe how you came to hold each opinion. Share your thoughts with at least three of your classmates.

Strong opinions that would be difficult to change (you will be asked to refer to these again in Activity 2):

1) _____
2) _____
3) _____

Activity 2
Look back at the three opinions you identified in Activity 1.

a) How would embracing the concept of "there's always more to know" help you to become more open-minded about one of these subjects?
b) How would "indexing" influence your thinking on this topic?
c) Are there instances or situations you can envision where you would modify your opinion just a little? If you imagined a middle-ground of gray between your strong opinion and the other side, what would it look like?

Activity 3
Practice the technique of Indexing by first identifying two groups to which you belong—athlete, artist, bartender, student, neighbor, etc.

a) List the things all members of each group are likely to have in common.
b) Now, list the ways in which you are different from other members of the group.
c) Compare your findings in these two categories—are you more or less similar than you imagined?

Activity 4
Form a group and discuss the following questions.

a) If every person is biased to some extent, is there such a thing as complete objectivity? Is it possible?
b) What would life be like if everyone were completely objective in his or her thinking?
c) Create a list of questions that might be useful to ask ourselves to ensure that we have considered multiple perspectives.

Activity 5

How does knowledge of past behavior affect your actions and attitudes toward someone? With your group members, discuss how you would respond to each of the following situations. Try to identify the factors that account for group member differences in how each situation was perceived and addressed.

1) A childcare provider has a criminal record.
2) A friend is repeatedly late even though she keeps promising she'll be on time.
3) A teacher has a reputation for playing favorites and giving low grades.
4) A child is known to be anxious and shy.
5) A supervisor takes his employees for drinks every Friday.

Activity 6

Form a group and take turns responding out loud to the following statements. At the end of each round, discuss your responses with group members. How do assumptions influence your thinking and behavior?

1) When a friend confides she is going to counseling, I assume...
2) When I see a very orderly desk, I assume...
3) When I meet a test pilot, I assume...
4) When I talk with someone who has no long-range goals, I assume...
5) When someone complains about nearly everything, I assume...
6) When I see someone with tattoos covering her body, I assume...

Assess Your Current Listening Behavior: Evaluating

Rate your *evaluating* on the following scale of 1 to 5.

_____5. I automatically ask myself questions about a speaker's credibility. It also helps me pay attention to any ethical issues in what she advocates. I am excellent at analyzing evidence and reasoning and recognizing emotional appeals. Listening with an open mind is another of my strengths.

_____4. I don't take things at face value. I enjoy analyzing what I hear and trying to figure out if the speaker really knows what he's talking about. Ethical issues are also important, although I don't always catch those. If you ask me, I'm pretty open-minded, too.

_____3. I'd like to assume that everyone has good intentions and isn't trying to take advantage of me, but I realize that's naïve so I do pay attention to evidence.

I know I should analyze a person's emotional appeals, but sometimes I just want to sit back and listen.

_____2. I find it difficult to both listen to the content of what someone is saying and to analyze their logic and appeals at the same time. It's a lot of work, and sometimes it takes the enjoyment out of listening. I'm not a particularly diligent critical listener.

_____1. I don't listen well to things that are all facts. If a speaker doesn't use emotional appeals, then they get boring and I stop listening. So, I guess I don't really analyze what I hear. I just react to things in the moment.

8

LISTEN TO RESPOND

Outcomes

You listen. Then what? You may have heard the saying that you "can't *not* communicate." It's true—silence, clearing your throat, looking away; each has a different meaning to the speaker about how his or her message was received, about how well you listened. Sometimes your response is unintentional—your facial expression communicates that you thought an idea was crazy but you didn't intend to share that perception. Regardless, the speaker—who now becomes the "listener"—can interpret what you say and do in any number of ways. If you want your communication exchange to be effective and if you want to accomplish your goals, managing your response becomes an important listening responsibility.

You'll likely find that you have what we call habitual responses, a particular way you react to a situation almost all the time. While this response may be working well for you, what happens when it doesn't?

In this section we emphasize the importance of developing behavioral flexibility, the ability to assess a communication situation and deliberately choose the way you react. Two styles of particular importance in facilitating effective listening are the assertive response, and non-defensive behavior. Remember, you are a stimulus to the other person—if your reaction isn't what they expect, it's likely they will change the way they respond as well.

Listening Outcome RS1: Provide Clear and Direct Feedback

It's easy to assume that someone "knows" what you think—that they realize they've done something really helpful and you're appreciative, or that something thoughtless that made you angry. We figure we don't need to create a potentially awkward situation by articulating our thoughts. Perhaps they didn't follow procedures, or they aren't keeping their end of an agreement. The truth is, however, that people are often clueless; they think everything is fine when, really, there's an issue that's not being addressed. As you can imagine, if you avoid the problem rather than confronting it, the situation never improves. You can think of feedback as a gift. Positive feedback can motivate and build self-esteem; constructive feedback can redirect someone's efforts and help them become increasingly effective.

Skills for Success

1. Follow the Rules of Constructive Feedback
Thinking about giving feedback may make you feel anxious or stressed. That's because it is often done poorly, creating defensiveness and harming relationships.

BOX 8.1 GUIDELINES FOR CONSTRUCTIVE FEEDBACK

Give Feedback Constructively

Make your purpose clear—don't leave the other person wondering what the conversation is going to be about.

Be specific and descriptive—give feedback on a specific behavior by providing facts that make your point clear and vivid. Try not to generalize.

Situation/behavior/impact—let the person know what impact his or her behavior has had; enable them to see why you felt feedback was appropriate.

Use non-judgmental language—the language you use and the attitude it communicates is important.

Make sure the person can respond to your feedback—the person receiving feedback needs to be able to change.

Create the appropriate setting—try never to give feedback in front of others; create a comfortable and private environment.

Ask the person if they would like you to give them feedback—feedback is more meaningful if it is solicited, not imposed.

Receive Feedback Constructively

Listen closely—there may be useful information about the way others perceive you.

Overcome the urge to be defensive—you may reject what the person has to say in the end, but allow yourself to receive the feedback and be open to the possibility that it may be correct.

Clarify anything that you do not understand—paraphrase what you think you heard and check to see that it is correct.

Constructive feedback, on the other hand, helps someone see themselves from another point of view and gives them direction for self-development and personal growth. Learning to provide constructive feedback takes mindful responses and practice, but it is well worth the effort. Box 8.1 lists the most important factors to keep in mind as you give valuable information to another person.

2. Learn to Solicit and Accept Feedback
It's always great to be congratulated and appreciated. Unfortunately, no one does everything right all the time—and everyone can benefit from a little help and new insights into how they might further improve.

Accepting constructive feedback is as important as giving it, especially if you are ready to accelerate your professional development. One proven way to respond when someone has a piece of often surprising information about your behavior is to ask probing questions. Find out everything you can about the person's perspective, ask for examples of the behavior, and make sure you agree on a positive path for the future.

3. Consider the Nonverbal Environment
Constructive feedback depends not only on what you say, but also the context in which it's provided. "Saving face" is important to all of us—no one likes to be embarrassed or singled out in front of friends and colleagues. Always make sure that the environment is appropriate for the situation; that means that it is private, that you can be seated relatively close to the other person, and that there are few distractions so you can focus your complete attention on the conversation.

Activities to Ensure Clear and Direct Feedback

Activity 1
Recall a recent lecture that you've heard, either in class or at a special event.

a) Assume that the speaker asked for your feedback.
b) Write at least five bullet points, providing constructive comments that would help her recognize both her strengths and areas for improvement.

Activity 2
Pair up with a classmate and take turns providing each other with constructive feedback. Use the following brief scenarios to begin.

Scenario A
You are helping a neighbor learn to swing a golf club. Change the following to reflect constructive feedback skills.

a) That is a terrible swing!
b) Your stance is all wrong—you can't balance if you are only on one foot.

c) Stop looking at the other golfers and pay attention to your own ball.
d) That baggy shirt doesn't help much and seems get bound up when you raise your arms.

Scenario B
You are having a hard time adjusting to your new apartment because of a number of issues you think should be resolved. Your landlord asks you for your feedback after the first two weeks. Change the following to reflect constructive skills.

a) The stove is a piece of junk—it only heats half the time.
b) We feel like we are taking our life in our hands whenever we climb that second flight of stairs.
c) The tenants right below us in 2B are inconsiderate jerks—they keep their stereo blasting day and night.
d) Our dishes are still on the floor, awaiting the cabinets you swore would arrive last week.

Activity 3
You've done the best job you can on the project report, but your supervisor seems impossible to please. Pair up with a classmate to role play the following situation. Respond to the criticism by *probing* and see what happens.

• I told Jamie you were lazy—your report was late.
• The report is short; I'm not convinced that you really analyzed all the data.
• Every good report has a cover page; this looks unprofessional.
• You didn't cite all of the sources I'm sure you must have used.

a) Did you find probing easy or difficult? Can you envision using it in the future?
b) Identify two personal situations in which probing may be an effective technique.

Activity 4
In a small group, discuss the following questions.

a) What impact does the way feedback is expressed have on an employee's performance?
b) How does constructive versus non-constructive feedback affect motivation and attitude?
c) In what situations can you see yourself giving feedback? Are there ways you can prepare for this opportunity?

Activity 5
Role models are helpful in a variety of ways.

a) Do you know someone who gives extraordinary feedback—information that is on target, relevant, constructive, and motivational?
b) What, exactly, does this person do that sets him apart?
c) Does your relationship with the person giving feedback influence how readily you accept it?
d) Does your relationship influence the type of feedback you receive? In what ways?

Listening Outcome RS2: Increase Behavioral Flexibility

Everyone has habits. While they can be useful in reducing stress and taking away the need to think about every decision, they can become so automatic that you don't even realize there are choices—other ways of doing things (see Box 8.2). If your interactions are going well and you are happy with the outcomes, then your habitual patterns of communication are serving you well. But when things change—when you encounter a new or novel situation—it is important that you have a back-up plan. Increasing your behavioral flexibility,

---

BOX 8.2 RESPONSE OPTIONS

You have choices about how you respond to a situation—lots of them! Which of the following do you frequently use?
A friend says to you, "I lost my car keys!"
Angry—"I'm sick of your absent-mindedness!"
Questioning—"Where did you drive last?"
Empathetic—"You sound distressed, I know how upsetting that can be."
Supportive—"Don't worry, I'll help you look and we'll find them."
Advisory—"Why don't you check on the car seat?"
Critical—"You certainly have trouble keeping track of things."
Assertive—"Just sit down and think for a few minutes before taking any action."
Sarcastic—"Again?!"
Disbelieving—"Didn't you just lose the keys yesterday, too?"
Silent—No response.
Defensive—"What, you think I took them?"
Sympathetic—"I am so very sorry. Poor you!"
Discounting—"Oh, by the way, I think it's your turn to do the dishes."

which means developing a range of skills to use when a new situation arises, can distinguish you from others who get "stuck" in a particular style or approach. Remember, too, that when you change your listening response, it will change the way others respond to you as well.

Skills for Success

1. Assess Your Behavioral Style and Preferences
First, try to be mindful of the way you respond to various situations. Do you use a similar response regardless of who you're talking with or where you are? A quick personal assessment of your behavioral preferences will help you identify your "go-to" response styles. It's important to do this with an open mind, as we aren't always in the best position to objectively assess our own behavior. After all, we're caught in a fleeting situation and things "just happen." What might be really helpful, then, is to ask the people who know you best to help you describe and identify the responses you use the most, and the situations in which you are most likely to be. . . predictable.

2. Deliberately Learn and Practice New Ways of Responding
Once you have an accurate understanding of how you respond, you are in a position to explore the wide range of potential options, asking yourself whether some of these styles might be more appropriate in certain situations than your current patterns. The more skills you acquire, the more your effectiveness increases as you match the needs of a particular situation with the most appropriate and high-impact response.

Activities to Increase Behavioral Flexibility

Activity 1
Review the list of response options in Box 8.2. Think about the way you respond to the following situations and then identify the style that best represents your current behavior. If you believe your response isn't predictable, indicate that as well.

1)   You aren't sure where the ticket line ends so you join what you think is the back; a stranger yells at you for "budging."
2)   One of your parents criticizes your appearance.
3)   A friend tries to convince you to go out when you know you should stay in and do homework.
4)   A salesperson is rude to you at checkout.
5)   You are ready to leave for a dinner reservation but your friend, as always, is running very late.
6)   A neighbor child throws your favorite baseball in the river.

You might share your choices with friends or classmates to see if they agree with your assessment!

Activity 2
A number of situations are described below. Provide—either orally or in writing—a response that would fit each of the possible categories. Then, indicate those responses that are "most like me" and those that are "something I would NEVER say!"

	Would Never Say			*Might Occasionally Say*				*Most Like Me*		
1) Your significant other won't speak to you.										
a) questioning	1	2	3	4	5	6	7	8	9	10
b) sarcastic	1	2	3	4	5	6	7	8	9	10
c) discounting	1	2	3	4	5	6	7	8	9	10
d) sympathetic	1	2	3	4	5	6	7	8	9	10
e) critical	1	2	3	4	5	6	7	8	9	10
2) A child gets hurt.										
a) angry	1	2	3	4	5	6	7	8	9	10
b) questioning	1	2	3	4	5	6	7	8	9	10
c) advisory	1	2	3	4	5	6	7	8	9	10
d) sympathetic	1	2	3	4	5	6	7	8	9	10
e) critical	1	2	3	4	5	6	7	8	9	10
3) Your friend loses her keys.										
a) questioning	1	2	3	4	5	6	7	8	9	10
b) sarcastic	1	2	3	4	5	6	7	8	9	10
c) advisory	1	2	3	4	5	6	7	8	9	10
d) discounting	1	2	3	4	5	6	7	8	9	10
e) supportive	1	2	3	4	5	6	7	8	9	10

Activity 3
With a group of your classmates, discuss the following questions.

a) Do your different roles—student, friend, employee, son or daughter—require different types of response styles?
b) In which situations do you feel most comfortable with your response? In what situations, and with whom, do you tend to use less-productive styles (criticism, advice, discounting, etc.)?
c) What does your communication partner do that helps you respond in positive and constructive ways?

Activity 4
Think about the following.

a) If you had one response you would like to further develop and use more, what would it be?
b) If you could choose one response that you would like to use less frequently, what would that be? How might you go about making these changes?
c) Look at the SMART goal section in Chapter 9 and create an action plan for change.

Activity 5
In some situations, your listening challenge is to respond in a manner that encourages other people to listen to you.

a) Describe one significant challenge in the workplace or another context where you have difficulty getting others to listen to you. Describe the specific situation, and the people involved, and explain why you don't believe *you* are always heard.
b) How does it feel when colleagues or family members don't listen to you? How do you respond when you feel your thoughts are discounted or ignored?
c) What specific components of the HURIER Listening Model are involved in this situation?
d) List three specific actions you can take to increase the likelihood that others will listen to you.

Listening Outcome RS3: Develop Assertive Skills

One style that is effective in numerous situations is called the assertive response. The reason it is so important to develop assertive skills is that they almost never come naturally—and yet they are one of the most useful and appropriate ways of responding to a number of difficult communication situations.

BOX 8.3 DEFINITION OF ASSERTIVE BEHAVIOR AND ASSERTIVE SITUATIONS

Assertive behavior enables a person to:

- act in their own best interests
- stand up for themself without feeling anxiety
- express honest feelings with confidence
- exercise personal rights without denying the rights of others

An *assertive response* can be helpful in the following situations:

- saying "no" when you want to
- receiving criticism
- giving criticism
- expressing feelings
- ending conversations
- giving others compliments
- stating ideas with impact
- stating personal needs
- initiating conversations
- not allowing others to make their problems your problems

When someone is assertive, they communicate in a clear, straightforward, and respectful manner. They gain credibility and project confidence not only through their words, but also through nonverbal behaviors such as direct eye contact, forward posture, and calm but forceful vocal cues (Box 8.3).

Your first task is to recognize assertive behavior when you hear it because one way to develop your personal style is to model it after someone you admire. Once you become familiar with both the verbal and nonverbal elements of assertive behavior, you can practice it in non-threatening situations. When you are confident of your skills, you can begin to address some of the troublesome listening situations that have not been resolved through other options. Keep in mind that just because the assertive response may be most appropriate in accomplishing your goals, it's not guaranteed to get the results you want in every situation. What does happen, however, is that you will have expressed yourself in a respectful, clear manner and have paved the way to a healthier and more productive relationship.

Skills for Success

1. Express Feelings Verbally

Sometimes an emotional response is appropriate; in fact, expressing emotions is important for healthy relationships and your own mental health. The way you express emotions, however, is key. After listening to what someone has to say, shouting at or insulting them—or responding with sarcasm or overt disbelief—may not be the most productive option. One of the most useful assertive skills is learning to verbalize the emotions that potentially create hard feelings or ignite further conflict. Emotions, then, become part of the content of your response rather than a separate, often destructive force. Instead of yelling, "Why didn't you tell me you were going to be late?!" you would make your anger part of your verbal message: "When I spend time waiting for you I become frustrated and upset because it keeps me from making progress on all the work I have to do. Please let me know if you're going to be late."

2. Say "No" by Using Broken Record

You likely recall times when you began with good intentions—when you said "no" to a friend who wanted to borrow your car, or to a salesperson who wanted you to buy something that cost more money than you could afford. But your friend keeps pushing, asks you why you can't lend him the car or join him at the show. That's when you feel things slipping—when you feel trapped and unable to get out of the situation.

Your first mistake here was to give reasons for your decision. As soon as you hear yourself saying, "I can't help you because..." the other person has ammunition to counter each objection. While some of your friends may respect your decision and your reasons, others might not be so understanding. The skill of *broken record* suggests that you simply continue, sincerely and perhaps with genuine regret, the simple phrase "I'm sorry but I just can't (let you take the car/stay out late that night/pay $150 for the show)." *Broken record* enables you to hold your position and still show concern or disappointment. While this response is not always appropriate, there are times when it is the most effective way to accomplish your goal and make your point.

3. Stand Up for Your Beliefs and Seek a Workable Compromise

Expressing your beliefs, even when they are unpopular, is another assertive goal. This response takes practice, because almost everyone likes to avoid conflict and to be seen as sharing the same views as their friends. When there is disagreement, however, you may be able to negotiate a compromise that maintains the essential elements of each position. Effective listening enables you to accurately understand what is important to your partner, and from there you are well-positioned to propose alternative solutions or a course of action that is satisfying to both parties—a *workable compromise*.

4. Handle Criticism through Negative Inquiry or Fogging

Negative inquiry is an under-utilized response that can be very effective when you feel you are being criticized unfairly. It is very similar to probing, a feedback strategy discussed earlier. Whereas probing is intended to solicit additional

---

BOX 8.4 STEPS TO ASSERTIVE BEHAVIOR

1) Identify your current response—what is your first reaction when confronted with a situation where assertive skills are required?
2) Think about your assertive needs and select one person or situation where you would like to increase your assertiveness.
3) Use positive self-talk; visualize yourself handling the situation in an effective, assertive manner.
4) Just do it!
5) Get feedback on the effectiveness of your efforts. If no one else was there, reflect on your skill and comfort with your assertive response.
6) How can you improve?

---

information to improve performance, *negative inquiry* is most often used when you feel you are being criticized unfairly.

First, acknowledge that you understand the other person's concern—perhaps by simply restating the issue. Then, instead of defending your position, ask for additional information and clarification. Try not to apologize or defend yourself—just keep asking questions. If possible, schedule a later time to resume your conversation after you have been able to consider the situation with a fresh perspective.

Fogging is applied in similar situations, but in this case you simply agree with what your communication partner says. Try not to justify, explain, clarify, or defend. Simply make statements such as "I can see how you may have thought that I acted prematurely. I know you would have waited longer before taking action on this case," or "You're right. I let down the team when I failed to finish up those visuals. I can tell that everyone is upset with my behavior." *Fogging* is useful in that the person giving criticism has nothing to react to—it allows them to become increasingly calm and rationale in their communication because you have eliminated the conflict. Regardless of the specific type of response you would like to develop, you can follow some simple steps to increase assertive skill (Box 8.4).

Activities to Develop Assertive Skills

Activity 1
There may be significant differences in how comfortable you are using assertive skills with different people.

a) Consider how easy or difficult it is for you to respond assertively when you communicate with the following:

    1) your significant other/spouse
    2) professors
    3) children
    4) classmates you don't know well
    5) good friends
    6) parents

b) What do you think explains differences in how you behave or how comfortable you feel expressing yourself assertively? What reaction do you anticipate? What outcome?

Activity 2
Think about the last time you became emotional in a conversation.

a) Are there emotions that you would like to express as part of the content of your message rather than demonstrating them indirectly through your word choices, voice, and other nonverbal cues?
b) When are you most satisfied with how you communicate emotions? Under what circumstances are you least satisfied?
c) In a small group of classmates, discuss how you typically communicate each of the following emotions as well as the circumstances under which you are likely to experience the emotion when you are listening:

    1. anger
    2. annoyance
    3. pain
    4. fear
    5. excitement
    6. frustration

d) Select one of the situations you've described and explain how the emotion could best be communicated assertively as part of your verbal response.

Activity 3
One way to develop assertive skills is to identify a role model, someone you admire for their ability to effectively communicate in a direct and assertive manner.

a) Who do you think has an effective assertive response? Describe his or her communication style and give an example of how assertive behavior was demonstrated. Why were you impressed?

b)   What can you learn about how to respond assertively by observing this person? What changes in your habitual response might you want to make?

Activity 4
Form a small group with your classmates. Assign one member to be the "borrower." This person will speak to each of the other group members in turn in an effort to get them to agree that he can borrow something. He might plead, beg, threaten—it's important for him to be forceful in making the request. Each of the other group members practices an assertive skill as they refuse to lend him the item:

* *broken record*
* *negative inquiry*
* *workable compromise*

a)   Discuss each person's effectiveness as they applied an assertive skill.
b)   Which skill seemed to be most effective in this situation?

Activity 5
Form a small group with your classmates and identify a familiar situation where accepting criticism is required.

a)   Determine the details of the situation.
b)   Choose two members to role play for the rest of the group using *fogging* as an assertive technique. Your exchange should last one to two minutes.
c)   Role play the situation again, or identify a new circumstance where someone is being criticized, and practice *negative inquiry* by role playing that response.
d)   Discuss the effectiveness of each response. When might it be useful and appropriate?
e)   Under what circumstances would an assertive response be ineffective or inappropriate?

Activity 6
Discuss the following questions.

a)   What would happen if suddenly everyone decided to become more assertive?
b)   Create, either individually or with your group, a set of guidelines or recommendations regarding when the assertive response is most appropriate, and when it's not.
c)   Are there some cultures where individuals are encouraged to be more or less assertive? How would you describe the United States? Japan? India? France?

Activity 7
Read the case below, *All Work and No Play*, and then discuss the questions that follow.

All Work and No Play

You supervise a highly competitive sales team. Everyone depends heavily on the administrative support that your organization provides. In fact, just six months ago, additional assistants were hired to take care of the heavy workload the sales team generated. Timeliness and accuracy are critical, as the sales associates have to have all of their estimates made and paperwork generated to close the deal.

Recently you noticed that the work is not being distributed evenly among the ten administrative assistants. In the past you assigned each sales rep to a specific assistant, but that resulted in complaints because it was clear some individuals were much faster and more accurate than their co-workers. Now the procedure requires sales reps to submit their work into one of three piles—urgent, important, or standard. Members of the administrative team pick up the assignment that is next in the queue and return it when the job is complete. This new system has created a great deal of frustration and complaints from the administrative assistants. Someone in your office is upset and expressing frustration about what they see as an unfair practice every day. It is apparent that those assistants who work more efficiently simply work harder and do more than their co-workers, but from the reports you receive it is unclear just who works and who loafs. Morale is at an all-time low and you know something needs to be done to address this issue.

a)   What are the listening challenges in this situation?
b)   What listening skills will be required to address the problem?
c)   What response style will be most effective?
d)   After you have determined an appropriate response, role play several of the interactions. Discuss.

Listening Outcome RS4: Create a Supportive Communication Climate

Your "listening response" matters. It not only indicates to the speaker that she has been heard. It also conveys a lot of information about who you are—your interests, attitudes, values, and personal characteristics. Since, as you know, you have nearly unlimited options, you want to make sure that you respond in a way that strengthens your relationship as well as accomplishes your task. You also want to present yourself as credible and trustworthy. The impression you create, and the judgments others make about you, are affected by how you respond to what you hear. If you respond in a manner that establishes good will, you'll discover that others will seek out your opinions and support you in a leadership role. Responses that encourage open and non-defensive behavior, particularly in the workplace, are recognized as a key to communication effectiveness.

Even if you respond in a clear and respectful manner, there's no guarantee that your communication partner will do the same. You are likely to encounter friends, colleagues, or even family members who respond in a defensive manner to the things you say. The problem is, when they become defensive they're not listening to you. Your ability to manage the communication encounter and facilitate effective listening will be a huge advantage in whatever situation you find yourself. It's only through effective listening that you can begin to create positive, healthy communication environments.

Skills for Success

1. Recognize Defensive Behavior
You'll know right away when someone is defensive. They'll refuse to listen. They'll become angry and illogical. In some cases, they'll even begin saying things you know aren't true. Defensive behavior is self-focused; a defensive person isn't able to look at the big picture or recognize someone else's point of view. He is quick to place blame—on someone else. Obviously, when this happens communication breaks down completely. That's why it's important for you to recognize the blocks to supportive communication and to develop responses that will reduce defensiveness and ensure a productive and honest exchange. Defensiveness affects not only individuals but teams, departments, and entire organizations.

2. Develop and Practice Supportive Responses
While there are a variety of ways to analyze defensive behavior, one of the most useful frameworks was proposed by Jack Gibb (2007). He suggests that we can view behavior on a defensive-supportive scale and work to reduce defensive responses by practicing more productive—what he calls "supportive"—skills. Look at the explanations provided in Box 8.5 and make sure you understand and can identify the behaviors described. Since we all have habitual ways of responding, it will take time and practice to change behaviors so that more effective listening takes place. By providing supportive responses, however, you will be reducing the defensiveness that keeps communicators focused on saving face and defending their position rather than on sharing information and working toward better understanding and improved relationships.

3. Create a Supportive Listening Environment
The physical environment in which communication occurs also affects your listening and the quality of your response. Recall a situation where you felt uncomfortable and were so focused on how cold you were, or how sterile the

BOX 8.5 FOSTER POSITIVE RELATIONSHIPS THROUGH YOUR SUPPORTIVE RESPONSE

When someone is defensive, they stop listening and focus on protecting themselves and their position. You can ensure a respectful, productive exchange by using a supportive approach that facilitates constructive dialogue and fosters a positive relationship.

Descriptive versus Evaluative Language

When you're judgmental, the other person readily becomes defensive. Judgmental language is characterized by words like "terrible," or "lazy," or "stupid."

Defensive: "You're a horrible team member. It's a good thing Karl was here to help us out."

Supportive: "I was frustrated when we needed your help and couldn't find you. Karl stepped in to take up the slack, but it was your job. It is important to let us know when you're going to leave."

Problem-Solving versus Placing Blame

When something goes wrong, the other person will be much more likely to work toward solutions if you approach the situation from a problem-solving orientation rather than placing blame.

Defensive: "Don't you care about whether we get this project finished? You were the one who had to go to that reunion last week, and it was a huge hardship for everyone."

Supportive: "You can probably tell our team isn't as agile as we could be, especially when unanticipated events arise. Let's have a brainstorming session tomorrow and see if we can find some efficiencies."

Empathy versus Indifference

When you listen with empathy and try to see the other person's point of view, you encourage honest, two-way communication. This approach is in contrast to indifference, an attitude of, "I don't care what you think" or "this is what I've decided to do; I don't need you to tell me anything."

Defensive: "I know you're car broke down. So now that you're finally here let's get started."

Supportive: "I'm sure it was frustrating to have your car break down like that. Since being on time is essential, let's talk about how you might prevent that problem from happening again."

Provisionalism versus Certainty

Comments made with the recognition that opinions or positions might change are much more likely to be accepted than statements made from a position of "I'm right. End of story."

Defensive: "We are not allowing Sandy to bring her two-year-old to class—that's ridiculous."

Supportive: "It doesn't seem to me that it's a good idea for Sandy to bring her two-year-old to class. What would happen if she started to cry?"

Honesty versus Manipulation

Most people appreciate honesty and become defensive and upset if they feel they are being manipulated, even if the issue is a small one.

Defensive: "Oh, come on. I know you're on a diet but I've really been looking forward to a night at the Piggy Bank. I don't know how you can disappoint me like this."

Supportive: "I would really like to go to the Piggy Bank tonight but I realize you are on a diet. Maybe we can get a menu and see if there's anything healthy that you would feel comfortable ordering."

environment was, or how far away from the speaker you were sitting, that you found yourself distracted. We often underestimate the impact that color, furniture, and other environmental features have on our ability to listen. Recall the variables that influence attention and apply those to your listening environment. Often there are a variety of things you can personally do to alter the setting and create a positive experience for participants.

Activities to Create a Supportive Communication Climate

Activity 1

Discuss the following questions with members of your group.

a) Under what circumstances do you become defensive? Is there someone who provokes a defensive response without even trying? Why do you suppose that's the case?
b) How does it affect your listening? What about your relationship?
c) What can you do to anticipate and avoid that response?

Activity 2

Think about the five defensive-supportive dimensions Gibb proposes and determine which one occurs most frequently in your personal interactions.

Describe in detail a situation where your communication partner became extremely defensive, and then answer the following questions.

a) Did you contribute to the situation that led to your partner's defensiveness?

b)   What did you say when your partner became defensive? Was it the most appropriate response you could have made, or did it escalate the situation?
c)   Were you able to reestablish a positive relationship?
d)   How might you respond to a difficult situation in the future to reduce the likelihood that defensiveness occurs? What response styles are most appropriate? Are you comfortable with them?

Activity 3
Pay special attention to the defensive encounters in which you participate.

a)   Keep a journal of what happened by analyzing both your response and your partner's behavior.
b)   For each interaction, set a specific goal for how you might handle the situation in a different manner the next time you communicate.
c)   After five or six entries, determine if you can identify new behaviors that might be developed and integrated into your everyday response patterns.
d)   How comfortable are you with conflict in general? What response do you usually choose?

Activity 4
Form a small group with your classmates. Select one of the defensive-supportive dimensions listed in Box 8.5 and identify a situation—from work, school, or family—where you can role play both defensive and supportive communication encounters.

a)   First, role play the scenario where one participant demonstrates defensive behavior.
b)   Then, keep the same situation but change the communication so that person now responds in a supportive manner.
c)   Discuss your observations. Select a second defensive-supportive dimension and repeat this process by first role playing the defensive communication and then repeating the dialogue, this time demonstrating supportive communication.
d)   What were some of the differences you noticed between the outcomes in the defensive versus the supportive interactions?
e)   How might your response have a lasting impact on your relationship?

Activity 5
Think about the importance of listening in the following situations, and the influence environment has on your ability to both listen well and respond supportively. For each setting, describe your ideal environment—the things you believe might make a positive impact on your communication and foster

listening effectiveness. Discuss and compare your ideas with other members of your group.

1) A small group meeting.
2) A classroom for 25 students.
3) A living room.
4) A birthday party for twelve six-year-olds.
5) A manager's office.
6) A massage parlor.

Activity 6
As a small group, select a common communication setting—a living room, meeting room, lounge, etc. Each member has three minutes to sketch the environment—placement of chairs and other furniture, selection of colors, lighting, and so forth. Exchange plans and examine your classmate's drawing.

a) How would this environment influence communication?
b) Does the placement of furniture suggest that all participants can listen effectively?
c) Are some positions more desirable than others? Why?

Activity 7
Often, the work environment and the people you work with can have a dramatic impact on your listening as well as on the response choices you make. Consider the situation in the following case, *Sophia's Good Ideas*, and the factors that influence the listening environment.

Sophia's Good Ideas
Sophia worked in the bakery department of a large grocery store. While she enjoyed her job, she was routinely embarrassed when customers complained about not having many of the standard baked goods available. She suggested to her supervisor several times that they keep track of sales and make sure that enough product was available, but nothing changed. Her friend Jose had similar issues. His job was to cut the meats and make sure they were packaged and ready to be purchased. Anyone going through the meat bins, however, would notice immediately that many packages were past the recommended date to be sold. Jose, too, had repeatedly mentioned this problem to his department manager.

Both employees were excited several months ago when the store ran an "employees with good ideas" event to identify service dissatisfiers and generate creative solutions to some of the main customer concerns. Both Sophia and Jose participated by explaining that customers felt checkout lines were long and that a self-checkout would alleviate much of the problem. It also seemed to them that there were a large number of older adults who would benefit from more help taking groceries out to their cars. Both Sophia and Jose felt that the event was a great idea, but since then nothing has been said about what issues were brought up or what suggestions were made for improvement. None of the store employees knew what, if anything, would be happening as a result of the effort. Sophia had even volunteered to help with any follow-up that needed to be done, but when she made the offer, she was told that it would have to be on the weekend, when she already had other commitments.

a)   Describe the store's listening environment in as much detail as possible.
b)   Identify the major obstacles you see to effective listening.
c)   If you were in Sophia's position, what would you do?
d)   In your group, make a list of suggestions regarding the specific action(s) that Sophia and Jose could take to be "heard" in this environment.

9
ACHIEVE THE LISTENING ADVANTAGE

The first two steps in benefiting from the Listening Advantage are to 1) identify the Listening Outcomes you want to achieve and then 2) set a specific path to reach your goal. As you look at the Listening Outcomes you have covered in this text—whether your interest is in all of them or a selected number—you can probably pick out those that will make the greatest difference in your listening effectiveness.

If your purpose is to improve your listening in a particular career, you will find one or more of the applications in Part III useful—read on! Ideas and cases for practice and discussion are provided for six careers: education, healthcare, helping professions, law, management, and the service industry. If your specific career isn't listed, one of the six applications will be so similar to your future professional goal that you can follow that path with confidence.

The Listening Outcomes you achieve will distinguish you from your friends and colleagues. As an effective listener you will be prepared to make better decisions, understand different perspectives, provide support to family and friends, and behave in ways that facilitate respectful, ethical, and productive communication.

Now it's time to review the process of setting SMART goals that was discussed in Chapter 2 (Box 2.2) and to create a specific action plan to achieve them. The lists of Listening Outcomes (see the Comprehensive Applications Table in Part III) will give you direction as you think back about your strengths and identify those behaviors that you can develop to realize a powerful Listening Advantage. The last column in the table provides a place for you to indicate the Listening Outcomes you are targeting.

Remember that SMART goals are specific, measurable, attainable, relevant, and time-bound. While there may be a number of Listening Outcomes you'd like to master, it's best to identify just one or two goals to work on at a time. Once you feel you've made progress, then you can add another goal to your list.

Changing your behavior to achieve or strengthen important Listening Outcomes is a process that will take time and commitment. But by now you know that it's well worth the effort! Your journey through the field of Listening Outcomes has been relatively short, but there's no doubt that you will be able to develop a number of new skills that will provide you with a strong Listening Advantage. Remember, too, that developing skills is an ongoing process. You will be amazed at how many behaviors you now recognize that you never noticed before and how, with focused effort, your listening will continue to improve.

Identify Your SMART Goals and Create an Action Plan

1. At the end of Chapters 3 through 7 (hearing, understanding, remembering, interpreting, and evaluating) you assessed your current listening behavior on a scale of 1–5. Record your ratings for each component on the lines below. Then, rank order the five components according to your perceived current skill level. If components have the same score, use your judgment to sequence them so that no two components have the same rank. This will help you identify those areas you would like to strengthen.

	Self-Score	Rank
a. Hearing	_____	_____
b. Understanding	_____	_____
c. Remembering	_____	_____
d. Interpreting	_____	_____
e. Evaluating	_____	_____

2. Now, create a SMART goal. See if you can incorporate all of the essential criteria—SMART—so that it will serve as a guide for strengthening or changing your behavior. Two examples of SMART goals are given below. Example 1: I will demonstrate stronger behavioral empathy when listening to a friend's personal problem. My behaviors will be that I maintain eye contact, lean forward, and avoid interrupting. I will measure my achievement when, after three weeks, I ask my friend if she felt like I was listening and interested in what she had to say.

Example 2: Every week for the next four weeks, when I am in a meeting with one of my direct-reports, I will end the meeting by saying, "Now if I understand you correctly, you said. . ." and I will paraphrase what was said to me. I will then check with that person to see if I have understood correctly by saying something like, "Do I have that correct?" I will review my progress weekly.

Now, write your goal! Just get it down on paper—there will be plenty of opportunities to modify it later.

3. Once you are satisfied with the SMART goal, form a small group and share your goal with a few of your classmates. Ask them for feedback regarding whether you have all of the components required to be SMART.

4. Keep a journal and record situations that relate to the behavior(s) you are targeting. In each case, note who was involved and whether you are satisfied with the way you responded. If you think you could have been more effective, no worries! Just keep focused, keep improving, and keep listening!

Practice Just a Little Bit More: Mini-Cases

1. In Someone Else's Shoes

The mother's perspective. You have three daughters, ages 6, 11, and 14. You and your husband agree that, as schedules become ever more hectic, it's important to use dinner time as an opportunity to relax and share the day's events. Your 6-year-old has no problem telling everyone what she did from the moment she got up in the morning. Your 11-year-old thinks that going around the table talking about your day is probably the "stupidest idea ever," but she responds, somewhat unenthusiastically, to specific questions. Manja, your oldest daughter, refuses to participate. Her expression says it all. Your husband becomes frustrated with the entire effort and particularly annoyed with Manja, blaming her attitude for making it impossible to have a positive experience.

The oldest daughter's perspective. As the oldest of three children, you feel you are always stuck with more work around the house than anyone else and you're often asked to look after your six-year-old sister. You know your parents are well-meaning but they think they can be friends with you, that they need to know everything that goes on in your life. It's not that you're hiding anything; you just don't care what they have to say and you certainly don't want to talk with them at the dinner table. Your mom had this great idea that it would be a "family share" time. No way. Your little sister, as always, is annoying and never listens to anyone. She's a spoiled attention-grabber and will go on endlessly about herself. Your dad only wants to hear about sports. He pretends he's interested in art projects and other activities, but he's not. You can tell he is totally tuned out. You need to get away from these awkward dinner experiences and are thinking about just staying in your room or going to a friend's house.

a. Where are the listening challenges?
b. What is contributing to the issues?
c. If you were in the mother's position, what would you do to achieve your goal of creating a comfortable, relaxing family experience at dinner where members listen to each other?

2. Help Wanted

Two of your good friends, Mia and Freddy, have been engaged for nearly three years but have finally set a date. Last night Mia came to see you in tears. She said that Freddy won't even discuss wedding plans. After waiting so long she is anxious to put some specifics in place. Although she's not particular, she wants to make sure that Freddy is on board with whatever is decided. Through sobs, she describes Freddy's reaction as "insensitive and selfish." Apparently, whenever she brought up wedding plans he changed the subject. In fact, he started reading the paper as she explained their choices of venues. After several unsuccessful attempts, she got her coat and headed to your place to vent.

a. What is the problem in this situation? What are the listening challenges?
b. If you were to give Mia some advice to help her accomplish her goal without alienating Freddy, what would you say?

3. Invisible

You have gotten to know another student, Jose, quite well. You have two classes together and have gone out for lunch a few times to prepare for upcoming exams. Jose lives in an apartment with three other students: Nadia, Jim, and Sasha. You passed Jose on campus a few minutes ago and he was with his apartment mates. He waved and said they were all going for a bite to eat and invited you to join them. You were the last to enter the restaurant and took a seat at the end of the table. You felt a bit awkward immediately since you only knew Jose, but you hoped that you would find things in common with his friends. Wrong. The others began immediately to discuss an issue they were having with the cable arrangement at their apartment and went on from there... Often they would all break out laughing. Not only were you unfamiliar with the topic, but they didn't speak so that you could even hear all of the conversation. Nadia, who was sitting next to you, was fully turned to face the other side of the table. The noise in the kitchen and from the other diners didn't help. After several attempts to join in the conversation, you just gave up. No one even looked in your direction. You began to feel as if you'd made a big mistake joining the group.

a. What listening challenges can you identify?
b. What do you think is the best response in this situation for someone who isn't being heard?

4. On the Planet

You love the vibe of the new restaurant where you're working evenings as a bartender. The bar attracts a young crowd along with business people stopping by for happy hour. The bar's slogan, "If it's on the planet, we have it!" celebrates its claim to provide patrons with any drink they can imagine. And that's the problem. Happy customers shout out drink orders and turn immediately to their conversations. Sometimes you get requests from across the room for several different drinks. When you turn to fill the order, you often have no idea what was said. While you're fine if someone is sitting at the bar alone and orders something unusual, you are lost when there are a number of orders together; you doubt you can remember the table let alone the drinks. Last night you messed up badly with some loyal, important regulars and your manager is threatening to let you go. While some of your customers take your mix-ups in stride and laugh about it, most of them become irritated and angry. They yell things like, "Could we get a real bartender in here please?!" or, "Hey lady, are you just deaf or are you stupid?"

a.   What listening problems are evident?
b.   What recommendation would you have for the bartender?

5. Need to Choose

You've worked at a co-ed summer camp in Maine for three years, and this year the director felt you would be the best person to make hiring decisions for new counselors. You were flattered and excited because you know how important it is to get the right people to work with the children ages 8–12. After hours of interviewing, you have two final applicants and now have a tough decision to make. The counselor would be responsible for a team of ten campers, taking them to the various craft stations, swimming, lunch, and any other special activities, making sure that they followed camp policies and stayed safe. Each counselor would also lead a project of their choosing.

Butch. Butch seemed introverted and didn't elaborate on the answers he provided. He explained that he had worked with children at the Boys' and Girls' Club where he grew up, and had gotten tremendous pleasure out of helping young people learn and grow. His mother passed when he was 12, so he looked to camp experiences for a sense of community and relationships. He didn't know what he would do for his special project, and seemed a bit uncomfortable with the thought of leading the team in a formal situation.

He mentioned that he had first-aid training and that he enjoyed cooking. At the end of the interview, when you asked if there was anything more he wanted to know, Butch asked about safety issues and if there were opportunities for the counselors to get together and discuss the campers.

Koti. Koti introduced herself as "part-native American"—and then added, "everyone always asks me which part!" followed by hysterical laughter. You were sure her love of the outdoors was genuine. She was animated and bubbly, couldn't stop talking about her wilderness camping trips and how she even started a fire without matches. She had already planned the project she wanted to do with the children, and assured you it would be their most memorable part of the summer. Although she had never worked at a camp or with children directly, she came from a family of 11 and had a "huge" extended family, which she said gave her more experience than anyone else. Her answers to your questions were brief, as she clearly had her own agenda for your meeting. At the end of the interview when you asked if there was anything more she wanted to know about the program, she couldn't think of anything.

a. Analyze the strengths and weaknesses of each applicant, focusing in part on their listening skills.
b. Who would make the best counselor? Support your decision with whatever evidence you have available. You might reflect on the ideas in "listening—evaluating messages."

6. *Cute Little Fishies*

> My photograph of the koi pond should have won. Sara got first place because she's always talking with the judges, always wiggling her way in so that people will pay attention to her. Her images are okay, but this time mine was better, much better. It was original, creative, interesting. You can see a stupid sunset every day.

Josh was clearly upset at the outcome of the photography contest, and nothing anyone said could convince him otherwise. The three judges had made the reason for their decision clear; in fact, they went to great lengths to provide a detailed assessment of the winning photograph and why it was chosen.

As they provided their explanation, Josh focused on tearing his entrance ticket into tiny little pieces and dropping them on the floor. Immediately following the judges' presentation was a reception for all participants. Josh wanted to just leave but his girlfriend convinced him to hang out. "Your picture was great, the judges had only positive things to say about it," Olivia reminded him as she grabbed his arm, steering him toward the refreshments. As they were getting drinks Sara came over to tell Josh how much she liked his koi pond. "It's so cute!" Sara gushed. "Cute little fishies." She didn't say more because her parents and others were trying to get pictures of her. Josh shook his head. "They just wanted a woman to win. That's it. Why do I even bother entering these things? I don't care what they say, it's never fair." Josh set down his glass and went out the door, hitting his fist hard against the wall as he left.

a. Analyze the situation in terms of listening behavior.
b. What were the major challenges to effective listening that arose?
c. Is there any way that Josh could have been compelled to listen—to the judges and others?

Recommended Reading for Part II

Anaza, N. A., Inyang, A. E., & Saavedra, J. L. (2018). Empathy and affect in B2B sales-person performance. *The Journal of Business & Industrial Marketing*, 33(1), 29–41.

Bello, S. (2018). Develop your emotional intelligence. *Engineering Progress*, 114(9), 46–52.

Bodie, G. D., Vickery, A. J., Cannava, K., & Jones, S. M. (2015). The role of "active listening" in informal helping conversations: Impact on perceptions of listener helpful-ness, sensitivity, and supportiveness and discloser emotional improvement. *Western Journal of Communication*, 79, 151–173.

Borella, E., Carretti, B., Meneghetti, C., & Carbone, E. (2017). Is working memory training in older adults sensitive to music? *Psychological Research*, 4, 1–17.

Brownell, J. (1992). Preparing students for multi-cultural environments: Listening as a key management competency. *Journal of Management Education*, 16(5), 80–92.

Brownell, J. (1993). Listening environment: A perspective. *Perspectives on Listening*, pp. 241–260. A. Wolvin & C. Coakley (eds). New York: Ablex Press.

Brownell, J. (1998). Creating strong listening environments: A key hospitality manage-ment task. *The International Journal of Contemporary Hospitality Management*, 6(3), 3–10.

Brownell, J. (2011). The listening fast track. *Cornell on Hospitality: How to be Successful in the Hospitality Industry*, pp. 37–51. A. Sturman, J. Corgel, & R. Verma (eds). Hoboken, NJ: John Wiley & Sons.

Brownell, J. & Wolvin, A. (2010). *What Every Student should Know about Listening*. Boston, MA: Pearson Education, Allyn and Bacon Publishers.

Dekeyser, M., Raes, F., Leijssen, M., Leysen, S., & Dewulf, D. (2008). Mindfulness skills and interpersonal behavior. *Personality and Individual Differences*, 44, 1235–1245.

Friedman, H. & Gerstein, M. (2018). Leading with compassion: The key to changing the organizational culture and achieving success. *Psychosociological Issues in Human Resource Management*, 4(1), 36–55.

Gibb, J. R. (2007). Defensive communication. *Communication Theory*, 2nd edn, pp. 201–212. C. D. Mortensen (ed.). New Brunswick, NJ: Transaction Publishers.

Gotsis, G. & Grimani, K. (2016). The role of servant leadership in fostering inclusive organizations. *The Journal of Management Development*, 35(8), 985–1010.

Gustafson, M. (2016). Leading by listening. *AgriMarketing*, 54(4), 40–44.

Hogan, T. P., Adlof, S. M., & Alonzo, C. N. (2014). On the importance of listening comprehension. *International Journal of Speaking & Listening Pathology*, 16(3), 199–207.

Kanter, B. (2017). Turning empathy inward. *Stanford Social Innovation Review*, 15(3), 70–72.

Nadler, S. & Simerly, R. L. (2006). The effect of listening on the formation of students' trust and commitment. *International Journal of Management*, 23(2), 215–221.

Parks, E. S. (2015). Listening with empathy in organizational communication. *Organiza-tion Development Journal*, 33(3), 9–22.

Riordan, C. M. (2014, January 16). Three ways leaders can listen with more empathy. *Harvard Business Review*. https://hbr.org/2014/01/three-ways-leaders-can-listen-with-more-empathy.

Roebuck, D., Bell, R. L., & Raina, R. (2016). Comparing perceived listening behavior differences between managers and non-managers. *International Journal of Business Communication*, 53(4), 485–518.

Sims, C. M. (2016). Do the big-five personality traits predict empathic listening and assertive communication? *International Journal of Listening*, 31(3), 163–188.

Timm, S. & Schroeder, B. L. (2000). Listening/nonverbal communication training. *International Journal of Listening*, 14(1), 7–12.

Turaga, R. (2017). Be silent to listen. *IUP Journal of Soft Skills*, 11(1), 48–58.

PART III

Listening Applications and Contexts

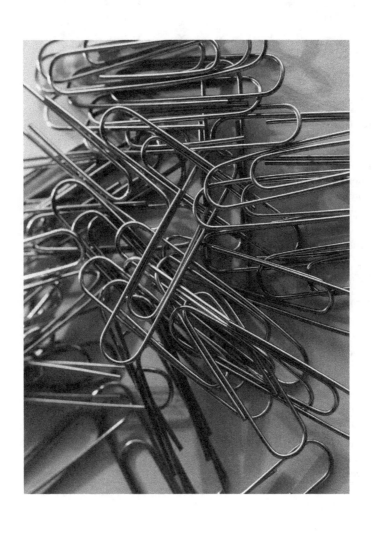

Comprehensive Applications Table

All Applications: Desired Listening Outcomes

	Education	Health care	Helping Profess	Legal	Manager and Leader	Service Industry	Your SMART Goals
Hearing Component: Desired Outcomes							
H1 Focus Attention on the Right Things				X	X		
H2 Don't Get Distracted	X	X	X	X			
H3 Hear the Message Accurately		X	X			X	
H4 Engage in Appreciative Listening							
Understanding Component: Desired Outcomes							
U1 Meet the Challenge of Individual Differences	X	X	X			X	
U2 Learn about Everything You Can	X	X	X	X	X	X	
U3 Zero In on Key Points				X			
U4 Reduce Interruptions		X	X				
Remembering Component: Desired Outcomes							
R1 Recognize Individual Factors that Affect Memory		X					

(Continued)

(Cont).

	Education	Health care	Helping Profess	Legal	Manager and Leader	Service Industry	Your SMART Goals
R2 Remember Names and Other Short-Term Memory Information	X		X	X		X	
R3 Improve Your Long-Term Memory	X						
R4 Reduce the Factors that Negatively Affect Memory	X				X	X	
Interpreting Component: Desired Outcomes							
I1 Develop Cognitive Empathy by Recognizing Individual Differences		X	X		X	X	
I2 Develop Your EQ and Social Sensitivity for Perceptive Empathy	X	X	X	X	X	X	
I3 Demonstrate Behavioral Empathy		X	X			X	
Evaluating Component: Desired Outcomes							
E1 Analyze Speaker Credibility				X			
E2 Determine the Ethical Dimensions of the Situation	X				X	X	X
E3 Analyze Evidence and Reasoning		X			X	X	
E4 Identify Emotional Appeals				X			
E5 Listen Objectively					X	X	

(Continued)

(Cont).

	Education	Health care	Helping Profess	Legal	Manager and Leader	Service Industry	Your SMART Goals
Responding Component: Desired Outcomes							
RS1 Provide Clear and Direct Feedback	X	X	X		X	X	
RS2 Increase Behavioral Flexibility	X		X	X		X	
RS3 Develop Assertive Skills	X	X			X	X	
RS4 Create a Supportive Communication Climate	X	X	X		X		
Listening Contexts							
Interpersonal	X	X	X	X	X	X	
Team	X	X	X	X	X	X	
Public	X				X		
Mediated	X	X		X	X	X	

LISTENING APPLICATION 1

Education

Applications 1, Table 1

Desired Listening Outcomes: Education

Hearing Component: Desired Outcomes	
H1 Focus Attention on the Right Things	
H2 Don't Get Distracted	X
H3 Hear the Message Accurately	
H4 Engage in Appreciative Listening	
Understanding Component: Desired Outcomes	
U1 Meet the Challenge of Individual Differences	X
U2 Learn about Everything You Can	X
U3 Zero In on Key Points	
U4 Reduce Interruptions	
Remembering Component: Desired Outcomes	
R1 Recognize Individual Factors that Affect Memory	
R2 Remember Names and Other Short-Term Memory Information	X
R3 Improve Your Long-Term Memory	X
R4 Reduce the Factors that Negatively Affect Memory	X

(*Continued*)

(Cont).

Desired Listening Outcomes: Education

Interpreting Component: Desired Outcomes
I1 Develop Cognitive Empathy by Recognizing Individual Differences
I2 Develop Your EQ and Social Sensitivity for Perceptive Empathy   X
I3 Demonstrate Behavioral Empathy

Evaluating Component: Desired Outcomes
E1 Analyze Speaker Credibility
E2 Determine the Ethical Dimensions of the Situation   X
E3 Analyze Evidence and Reasoning
E4 Identify Emotional Appeals
E5 Listen Objectively

Responding Component: Desired Outcomes
RS1 Provide Clear and Direct Feedback   X
RS2 Increase Behavioral Flexibility   X
RS3 Develop Assertive Skills   X
RS4 Create a Supportive Communication Climate   X

Listening Contexts
Interpersonal   X
Team   X
Public   X
Mediated   X

Listening in Educational Environments

As a student, you may think that you are the one with listening challenges. You spend much of your time listening to lectures, listening to instructions and directions, listening to your parents when they call. Educators, however, also have significant listening responsibilities both in and outside of the classroom. Many educators focus primarily on their speaking abilities and platform skills, thinking that those competencies are most essential to their job. It's easy for them to underestimate the important role listening plays in instructional effectiveness and the larger student experience. Regardless of whether your interest is in pre-school, elementary, secondary, or post-secondary education, your listening can have a huge impact on your ability to help students learn. The most effective educators respond to students' interests and special needs; they listen to individual concerns as they mentor and coach. They individualize instruction to the extent possible so that every student has opportunities to realize her potential. They have an accurate sense of how to facilitate learning because they listen with curiosity and an open mind.

Listening Challenges in Educational Environments

An educator's job is multi-faceted, and listening challenges can arise in nearly every aspect of his or her daily activities. Teachers listen to determine what their students know and what they need to know. They have to interact with sensitivity and compassion, yet be able to make difficult judgments and even more difficult decisions. Teachers listen to create supportive classroom environments; they often struggle to be fair and consistent. It is clear that their listening challenges extend out of the specific classroom context to less-formal student and parent interactions. The internet and other technologies pose additional listening opportunities and listening challenges.

Key Listening Outcomes

1) Develop short-and long-term memory.
2) Ask key questions for understanding.
3) Check your perceptions.

Contexts: Interpersonal, team, public, mediated.

Cases in Education

Case 1. Stories from the Trenches

You've enjoyed interacting with children since high school, and you find elementary school teaching challenging but highly rewarding. As you stand in the middle of the playground, two of your first-grade students come running up to you, one with a bloody nose.

"She hit me for nothing," Colin yells as they approach, blood streaming from his nose. "I was on the swing and she just came up and hit me."

"Did not," Maggie counters, swinging at him again. "You're lying. I was looking at my cell and you jumped off the swing right on top of me and pushed me down!" She starts to cry. "He's always mean to me! He's always pushing me!"

"No way," Colin insists, holding a tissue up to his face. "She gets away with everything 'cause she's a girl."

1) What are your listening challenges?
2) How do you get to the "truth" of the situation?

3) What is your best outcome?
4) What listening skills do you need?

Case 2. Listening Online

Experience in the classroom really doesn't prepare you for facilitating online classes. You've offered the same online course, "Effective job search strategies," twice now. When students complete the course they evaluate the instruction online. You were troubled with the feedback you received from the first offering, but now, looking at the feedback from your second iteration, you are even more concerned that they just "don't get it." You can't help feeling annoyed and upset. After all of your hard work transforming materials to an online format, the students have virtually ignored your guidelines, saying things like, "Instructions unclear," and "Important topics missing." Do they know what they need? That's why they're taking the class! As you read through the comments you become increasingly depressed.

1) What are the challenges of online communication and distance learning?
2) What is the most productive response you could make to the feedback you've received?
3) What specific actions might be taken?
4) What key "listening" skills will be most useful?

Case 3. Feel the Spirit

Ricki hasn't been doing well in school. You have the feeling that his misbehavior and lack of concentration are longstanding problems. In fact, you pulled his records in anticipation of the upcoming parent–teacher conference and realized that his parents have been given, and have ignored, the same messages for three consecutive years now. Your turn!

After greeting the Vermas, you get down to business. Your plan is to be straightforward about your concerns. "Mrs. Verma, I'm concerned because I don't feel that Ricki is getting as much value as he could from his classes. He seems distracted and, to be honest, he distracts many of his classmates as well."

"Yes, Ricki is an active, inquisitive child!" Mrs. Verma goes on to explain, "We love that about him. He is never quiet, always exploring and testing. He was brought up to be his own person and to think for himself."

You take a deep breath and continue.

> He is inquisitive, that's good. But he doesn't understand boundaries, he doesn't consider the other children and the need to work collaboratively. We have not been successful getting him to work on a team project or

finish a story. He knocks over things the other children build. He deliberately yells when I am reading to the class. They get upset with him, and that makes it even more difficult for him to fit in.

"Fit in?!" Mr. Verma repeats.

You're not listening to us. That is the trouble, precisely. All you educators think about is squashing a child's spirit and creativity so they will "fit in." Exactly. We do not want Ricki to fit in. You just need to get to know him rather than assuming that he is just like all your other little compliant robots.

1) Analyze the conflict and identify the listening challenges each party is confronting.
2) How might you approach the situation to turn it into a win-win?
3) What listening skills would be particularly important to develop and apply:

   a) for you?
   b) for Mr. and Mrs. Verma?

4) What realistic outcome might you expect?

Case 4. You Can Name It

You use a lot of case studies, and class discussions are one of the most enjoyable aspects of teaching. You always feel you learn a lot about your students from hearing their perceptions and ideas about how to approach various course content-related problems.

This morning you led a lively discussion related to business ethics. While the discussion itself went well, you twice called a student by the wrong name. During the first few weeks of class you tell yourself that, with nearly 40 students, mistakes like that will happen. Now, however, more than two months into the course, you know your students are somewhat offended when you call them by the wrong name or simply can't recall their name. In addition, you've always thought it was important to link ideas from one topic to the next but, again, your efforts have recently backfired. You were proud of yourself for recalling that one of your students worked in a family business. You thought it was Jai, but when you commented to Jai that his father might find some of the principles useful, he shook his head and motioned to Jake. You feel you are losing credibility with the entire class.

1) What are the listening challenges you face in this situation?
2) What are some of the factors that may be causing these problems?

3)   Identify the specific listening skills that would be most useful in addressing the issues you are experiencing.

Education: If You Were There

Scenario 1. Multi-Tasking

You teach in a progressive high school where students are highly motivated and college-bound. This year you've noticed a dramatic increase in cell phone use, especially texting during the class period. There are times when you know students are texting but they are so skilled that it's difficult to know exactly when they are using their cell. You know that multi-tasking affects their listening, but you're unsure what to do about it. Occasionally you ask a question and a student will struggle to "reconnect" with the discussion—you are pretty sure that it's because they were online. You want to maintain a positive relationship with your students and let them know you understand their lifestyle, but at the same time you feel they are in class to learn the course content. You've heard arguments for creating strict policies about the use of cell phones on one hand, and arguments for ignoring the situation on the other.

a.   How seriously do you think this behavior affects students' listening in class?
b.   What should you do?
c.   Role play a situation where you speak to a student who you think has been texting.

Scenario 2. Just Want to Be Heard

You try hard to create an inclusive environment for your students, but in one of your classes you are finding it particularly difficult. You have two special-needs students who go to a separate morning program but join your class later in the day. The biggest problem is that their classmates don't listen to them; in fact, their peers respond with total indifference. A recent assignment required that each student speak for several minutes. While classmates cheered and were generally supportive of one another, they became disinterested and discourteous when one of the special-needs students spoke. While his speech was hesitant and at times difficult to understand, you felt that this was an opportunity that would improve his self-esteem if only his classmates would give him their attention.

a.   What are your goals in this situation?
b.   What actions should you take to achieve them?
c.   Role play the scenario where you address this situation.

LISTENING APPLICATION 2

Healthcare

Applications 2, Table 2

Desired Listening Outcomes: Healthcare

Hearing Component: Desired Outcomes

H1 Focus Attention on the Right Things	
H2 Don't Get Distracted	X
H3 Hear the Message Accurately	X
H4 Engage in Appreciative Listening	

Understanding Component: Desired Outcomes

U1 Meet the Challenge of Individual Differences	X
U2 Learn about Everything You Can	X
U3 Zero In on Key Points	
U4 Reduce Interruptions	X

Remembering Component: Desired Outcomes

R1 Recognize Individual Factors that Affect Memory	X
R2 Remember Names and Other Short-Term Memory Information	
R3 Improve Your Long-Term Memory	
R4 Reduce the Factors that Negatively Affect Memory	

(Continued)

(Cont).

Desired Listening Outcomes: Healthcare

Interpreting Component: Desired Outcomes

I1 Develop Cognitive Empathy by Recognizing Individual Differences   X
I2 Develop Your EQ and Social Sensitivity for Perceptive Empathy   X
I3 Demonstrate Behavioral Empathy   X

Evaluating Component: Desired Outcomes

E1 Analyze Speaker Credibility
E2 Determine the Ethical Dimensions of the Situation
E3 Analyze Evidence and Reasoning   X
E4 Identify Emotional Appeals
E5 Listen Objectively

Responding Component: Desired Outcomes

RS1 Provide Clear and Direct Feedback   X
RS2 Increase Behavioral Flexibility
RS3 Develop Assertive Skills   X
RS4 Create a Supportive Communication Climate   X

Listening Contexts

Interpersonal   X
Team   X
Public
Mediated   X

Listening in the Healthcare Environment

Providing care and support to someone who needs your help can be immensely rewarding. We've all taken care of a loved one at some point in time, or someone who isn't feeling well or who can't do things for themselves. It can also be exhausting and overwhelming. Care givers may suffer from stress, overload, or even depression. Whether the situation is personal or professional, whether in a doctor's office or a senior adult's residence, listening is essential in order to provide the right type of assistance or intervention. Each person is unique; each healthcare situation is different. Thoughtful listening will not only ensure that you do the right thing—it will also help to establish the trust and good-will needed for a strong patient–provider relationship. In many healthcare settings, you are key to ensuring that another person receives timely and appropriate care.

Listening Challenges in the Healthcare Environment

While patients may do a lot of talking, they often aren't clear about what is really going on. They are likely to focus on aspects of the situation that may not be as useful in helping you determine their needs. Part of your job, then, is to draw them out in ways that enable your patients to provide the most relevant information. When patients are fearful, worried, and emotional about their wellness, listening is the most important skill healthcare providers can demonstrate in providing support and helping them through their immediate situation. Emotions tend to interfere with effective listening so, as the healthcare provider, your job becomes even more difficult as your client feels upset, threatened, or intimidated.

Key Listening Outcomes

1) Hear the right information.
2) Know what to ask.
3) Listen beyond words to emotional states.

Contexts: Interpersonal, team, mediated.

Cases in Healthcare

Case 1. Just Do It

"I don't care what he tells you, he must eat something at noon every day. You have to find a way to get him to cooperate, period."

This was your second meeting with Mr. Sweeney's daughter, and it was not going well. You have coordinated his care for nearly two months, and his care giver has worked hard to establish a trusting and respectful relationship with her client. Getting him to eat is challenging but, when given some flexibility, she has been successful every day.

"In addition," his daughter added,

> I have a schedule I'd like followed for his daily routines. We will cut out the videos and substituted readings. He never liked watching TV and I'm sure it is much better for his mind if someone reads to him. I'd like to go over my list of requirements and some of the other changes that need to be made to his care.

As she spoke she reached into her purse and pulled out her notes. "Oh yes, there are a number of complications with his medications and it is absolutely essential that everyone on his care team understands exactly what he takes and when to administer each medicine."

1) What listening challenges do you anticipate for yourself?
2) What listening skills will you need to provide excellent care to Mr. Sweeney?
3) What listening skills will you need in order to develop a working relationship with Mr. Sweeney's daughter?
4) What factors are preventing Mr. Sweeney's daughter from listening?
5) What can you do to ensure effective communication among Mr. Sweeney, his family, and care givers?

Case 2. Don't Ask, Don't Tell

You love your job as a nurse in a small primary-care office, but it's difficult not to become frustrated when patients don't seem to trust you with key information. Your guess is that they want to wait to talk with the doctor, and see you as a gate-keeper, someone who may or may not pass along important information. Jan Daily is a good example. When she got into the examination room you found that she was running a fever of 102 and her blood pressure was considerably higher than normal. When you asked her questions about her medications, exactly how she felt, and tried to gather other pertinent information, she would barely respond. She would just stare, or look away, and it was difficult to hear her even when she did speak. You always felt that you could be much more helpful if you could only get better information in your pre-screening. You think of yourself as a good listener, it's just that no one will talk to you!

1) What are your listening challenges in this situation?
2) What do you think is the cause of these problems?
3) What specific listening skills might you develop to better accomplish your goals?

Case 3. More than Enough

As a primary-care doctor you pride yourself on getting the right information and making an accurate diagnosis. One situation that you have been experiencing with increasing frequency is when an older adult brings in another family member to his appointment. Yesterday there was a good example of this issue when the Pasquales came in together to see you.

You began: "So, Mr. Pasquale, how long have you been having pain in your side?" Mrs. Pasquale immediately responded to your question.

> He complains constantly. First, he says it is in his side, then he says it's in his stomach. I don't know why it moves around so much but he hasn't been able to do any chores and our house is getting to be a mess!

"And how long has this been going on?" you ask again.

"So it moves around," John huffs. "I told you I didn't need to see a doctor. It will probably just go away on its own."

"No," Mrs. Pasquale chimes in, "It is not going away and something like this needs to be looked at. You are constantly complaining. You even told your brother about it last night. You never tell your brother anything about your health."

"Yeah, it hurts quite a lot sometimes, especially when I go to do chores in the barn," John admitted.

"He says it is a sharp stabbing pain. Except at night. At night, he says, it aches, at least sometimes it does—and then I tell him to roll over and that seems to help," Mrs. Pasquale adds.

"It's not sharp," Mr. Pasquale asserted. "I never said it was a sharp pain. You make things up."

1) Identify the listening challenges in this situation.
2) What can you do to facilitate effective listening by all parties involved?
3) What are the most useful listening skills in this situation?
4) What is your listening goal? What would you like to see as the outcome of this appointment?

Case 4. Easy Come, Easy Go

You work as a nurse on the second shift at a large hospital. There have been so many changes and orders that record-keeping has become increasingly stressful, and valuable time is needed to be spent filling out "Transition" forms. Many of your colleagues neglected this responsibility completely, or provided such limited information that it was useless to the person taking over on the next shift. Since everyone was complaining, your supervisor suggested a brief meeting at the end of each shift so that information could be passed on and any issues discussed.

Rohit, who most often had the day shift, was just leaving as you sat down in the office. You felt annoyed since it was not unusual for him to just take off, leaving you to figure out whether your patients had their medications, what they had eaten, and other care issues.

Still standing, you ask Rohit to give you an overview of where things stood.

"Same as always," he said as he got his coat. "Everything is fine."

"What about Sasha?" you ask. "Is she back on a regular diet?"

"Just look at her chart from yesterday," Rohit offered. "You'll see if anything has changed."

"But I thought she had to have some new medications to deal with her digestive issues. The doctor mentioned that the last time he checked in."

"Oh, that's right," Rohit now recalled. "Sasha is taking some additional pills. They should be listed on her chart. Just look at the chart."

"Is she fighting her meds? Last night she threw the cup of pills and they went all over the floor."

"Don't know," Rohit replied. "Tommy did that round this morning and he's gone."

"What else should I know about the patients on our wing?" you ask, becoming even more upset.

"Let's see… can you walk me to the elevator? I have an appointment and I have to get going," Rohit said as he began his way down the hall.

1) What are the listening challenges that emerge in this situation?
2) What might be causing them?
3) What actions do you recommend to address these issues?
4) What specific listening skills would be most useful?

Healthcare: If You Were There

Scenario 1. What You See is What You Get

You work with Dr. Jenna Roma and have the highest respect for her expertise and patient focus. She is dedicated to her patients and always has their best interests in mind. That's why you were particularly shocked and upset when you were surfing the web and happened to come across some patient ratings and reviews. While you knew that she was struggling to develop a patient base, you attributed it to the fact that she was young and some people associated experience with expertise. Reading the reviews, you realize that the issue was her manner. Patients wrote things like, "The doctor looks like she hates her work," and "Dr. Roma couldn't care less about her patients. She asks questions, but doesn't seem to care what you say."

You're not sure whether to "listen" to these reviews and take some action, or whether to let it go and hope that at some point Dr. Roma will see that there's a problem with her lack of perceived empathy.

a. What do you see as the most productive action on your part? How can you intervene to be helpful?
b. What risks are involved—what would be the worst-case scenario?
c. Role play a conversation that you might have with Dr. Roma.

Scenario 2. Connection Lost

One of the most difficult things a doctor does is give a patient bad news. As a nurse in an assisted-living facility, you are often present when the doctor has a serious conversation with a patient. In this case, it's Maggie Sanders, who has been in assisted living for nearly three years but who now has to be moved to a dementia unit. With increasing frequency she has gotten lost on her way to the dining room, forgotten her medications, and taken other residents' clothes from the laundry room. As Dr. Ricci patiently explains the situation to her, Maggie begins shaking her head and accusing him of making up stories and "not liking her."

"It's just not true. Those things are just not true," Maggie forcefully responded. "I take my medications every day. I know exactly what I need. I don't know who told you I forget. I am just fine."

Dr. Ricci repeated, again, that the move was best for her and that he would continue to see her; he was not going to leave her with someone new.

"Well," Maggie seemed calmer and more relaxed, "I know this move isn't going to happen. I belong right here. Thank you so much for coming to visit me."

You realize that Dr. Ricci's message wasn't really "heard."

a.　What listening challenges can you identify?

b.　What do you do—what is your responsibility as a care provider?

c.　Role play your discussion with the patient.

d.　Assume you also believe you should talk with the doctor. Role play that conversation.

LISTENING APPLICATION 3

The Helping Professions

Applications 3, Table 3

Desired Listening Outcomes: Helping Professions

Hearing Component: Desired Outcomes	
H1 Focus Attention on the Right Things	
H2 Don't Get Distracted	X
H3 Hear the Message Accurately	X
H4 Engage in Appreciative Listening	
Understanding Component: Desired Outcomes	
U1 Meet the Challenge of Individual Differences	X
U2 Learn about Everything You Can	X
U3 Zero In on Key Points	
U4 Reduce Interruptions	X
Remembering Component: Desired Outcomes	
R1 Recognize Individual Factors that Affect Memory	
R2 Remember Names and Other Short-Term Memory Information	X
R3 Improve Your Long-Term Memory	
R4 Reduce the Factors that Negatively Affect Memory	

(*Continued*)

(Cont).

Desired Listening Outcomes: Helping Professions

Interpreting Component: Desired Outcomes

I1 Develop Cognitive Empathy by Recognizing Individual Differences	X
I2 Develop Your EQ and Social Sensitivity for Perceptive Empathy	X
I3 Demonstrate Behavioral Empathy	X

Evaluating Component: Desired Outcomes

E1 Analyze Speaker Credibility

E2 Determine the Ethical Dimensions of the Situation

E3 Analyze Evidence and Reasoning

E4 Identify Emotional Appeals

E5 Listen Objectively

Responding Component: Desired Outcomes

RS1 Provide Clear and Direct Feedback	X
RS2 Increase Behavioral Flexibility	X
RS3 Develop Assertive Skills	
RS4 Create a Supportive Communication Climate	X

Listening Contexts

Interpersonal	X
Team	X
Public	
Mediated	

Listening in the Helping Professions

In some contexts, like a counseling or coaching session, listening is the most important thing you can do to support the person who has sought your help. Listening first and effectively is essential to your ability to provide guidance or comfort to a friend, colleague, or client. Unless you completely understand the person speaking, there's no way you can facilitate her well-being. In such situations, the act of listening itself can be therapeutic.

The person's emotional response becomes key to understanding the entire person and to providing the response needed to move toward wellness and health. A strong and trusting relationship with your client is also essential if she is to feel comfortable disclosing the type of information needed to fully explore her concerns.

Listening Challenges in the Helping Professions

Often, individuals who seek help are looking for answers; many clients will want you to tell them what to do. They have, as might be expected, only seen the situation from their own perspective. As a listener, one of your responsibilities is to help your client come to his own conclusions and examine the situation more objectively so that good decisions can be made regarding how best to move forward. In some cases, clients are angry and unable to reflect on the situation in productive ways. Often, they want to take actions that are inappropriate or premature. You play a critical role in guiding their strategy and facilitating their recovery.

Key Listening Outcomes

1) Listen nonjudgmentally.
2) Demonstrate behavioral empathy.
3) Develop a trusting relationship.

Common context: Interpersonal, team.

Cases in the Helping Professions

Case 1. It's Me, Not You

"Maria, I can't help you unless you share your thoughts with me." You usually find your clients speak continuously, but Maria has been reluctant to give you much information during her first few sessions.

"You don't know me. I only talk with people I know," Maria responded in a hushed, almost inaudible voice.

"Okay," I said quietly. "Then help me get to know you better."

> I don't like counseling. There's nothing wrong with me. I have to come here and talk with you. You're getting paid for this, I'm not. There's probably something wrong with you, too. No one will listen to me or find out what I want. Everyone just tells me what to do and tells me what I need. They treat me with disrespect and there's nothing I can do. I'm not talking anymore.

Her voice was muffled by her hand, and she spoke with an accent which made her even more difficult to understand. You wanted to help, but you're not sure what approach to take.

1) What listening challenges does this situation present? Describe each in detail.

2) Describe your goals for this session—what do you hope to accomplish?
3) What listening skills will be of most use as you work to help Maria?

Case 2. It's All About Me

You've always taken pride in helping high-potential employees along a career ladder and witnessing the success they achieve through their hard work, exceptional skills, and sound decision-making. You consider yourself an excellent mentor and, as such, you chose to work only with employees you feel will benefit from your guidance. Rohit, however, may have been a poor choice. You've spent hours talking with him, both at work and elsewhere. At first you thought he was responding but lately you've seen signs that you find troubling. Yesterday, for instance, you had a meeting scheduled but, less than an hour before it was to start, you got an email that read, "Hey, something's come up—catch you later." During your last several sessions Rohit just wanted to talk about all his current accomplishments, how some of his colleagues were jealous and how he was going to "show them" by making sure he was recognized and "leaving the rest of them in the dust." He seemed much more interested in rambling on about his achievements than listening to any wisdom you might share. In fact, as he talked on and on you began to lose interest entirely and started thinking about how you were going to negotiate a new deadline on a current project.

1) What listening challenges can you identify in this situation—both yours and your mentee's?
2) What listening skills are needed by each of you?
3) Analyze the situation and determine what your goal might be going forward.
4) Propose a realistic course of action to achieve your goal.

Case 3. Looking Up

You've always wanted to work with children, and your job as a child advocate for the Department of Social Services gives you a chance to make a difference in the lives of children in need. At the moment, you are sitting with Manuel, a seven-year-old who was just removed from his drug-addicted mother and will soon be placed in foster care. Your job is to find out as much as you can in order to make the best placement possible.

You begin by asking Manuel what he likes to do. Your first question doesn't get a response, and it is difficult to tell what he is thinking because he is staring up in the air with little expression.

You try again to create some sort of rapport. "What do you see up there?" you ask.

"My mom likes blue," Manuel whispers.

You are encouraged by his response. This is a start.

"Do you like blue, too?" You ask.

"My mom gets angry when I talk to strangers," Manuel continues.

You aren't sure where the conversation will lead, but you are hopeful that you will be able to make a connection with the child and provide the help he needs.

1)   What listening challenges arise in this situation?
2)   What are your listening concerns?
3)   What listening skills are particularly important to accomplishing your goals?

Case 4. Who Has the Problem?

Ever since you can remember, you've loved soccer. First you just kicked a ball around at a local park, and then you played in school on the travel team and even reached the state championships in high school. Now you're coaching a college sport and love every minute of it or... almost. This year you've had a particularly rowdy team. Several members have been penalized for their behavior on the field, and recently you've had issues with team members calling each other names and shoving their teammates in the locker room.

Marty, in his second year playing, has been particularly abusive and volatile. After he pushes another team member into the bench and calls him names, you decide it's time to take stronger action. You pride yourself on being a coach who not only cares about the game, but also about the players.

When Marty enters your office you can tell he has a chip on his shoulder. He swings a leg over the back of the chair and looks down at you from a standing position. You motion him to sit, and once he is settled you begin the conversation.

"Tell me what's going on, Marty," you ask as calmly as you can. "You're a good player, we need you on the team, but lately you've been disrespectful to your teammates and to me. That has to end. You're hurting morale and causing a lot of anxiety among the other players."

"It's all me. It's always my fault," Marty stood up again. "You have no idea. No clue."

"Why don't you explain it to me then?"

"Why don't you just stop pretending to care about my situation and kick me off the team?" Marty yelled. "You're a sorry excuse for a coach. You may have all those other idiots fooled, but not me. You're the one who has the problem."

1)   What listening challenges arise in your exchange with Marty?
2)   What are your listening goals when you call him in to talk? Do they change during the conversation?

3)   What listening skills are particularly important to accomplishing your goals?
4)   Is it important to listen, regardless of the situation?

The Helping Professions: If You Were There

Scenario 1. It Takes Two

You have always been optimistic about the ability of a skilled counselor to help clients change dysfunctional behaviors and lead a happier, healthier life. At the moment, you are in a meeting with a husband and wife who have come to you for help strengthening their marriage. It seems clear that they agreed to see you just to please their family. The two of them have very different views on a number of important issues, and you would love to help them address and resolve these conflicts. As someone who is single, you feel a bit awkward giving them marriage advice and have tried to help them explore issues by asking questions. Unfortunately, your plan is not working as you expected; your questions have only led to yelling, name-calling, and defensiveness. This couple came to you for help, yet they seem hostile and definitely unable—or unwilling—to see their partner's perspective. In fact, as you listen you question whether they really want to find a compromise on their issues.

a.   What listening challenges can you identify?
b.   What would you do—what approach might be most effective if your goal is to facilitate listening?
c.   Role play the counseling interview with two of your classmates. First, role play as the above situation is described. Then, role play a second time as you work to facilitate effective listening.

Scenario 2. Need a Little Respect

There still seems to be a stigma regarding the need for counseling, which you find frustrating and unfair. You work with distressed children in a large school district in Utah, and you know that the children you see get teased and even ignored by their peers. In fact, if a classmate asks a child if they work with you, the child will often lie and insist that they aren't "one of those" students. You are convinced that if everyone better understood what you do and how common the issues are that you address, they would recognize how important your job is. You have made several attempts to educate children so that they will have a more positive view of therapy. Unfortunately, this is not a topic that they are willing to rethink or take seriously. Whenever you speak to a class about the issue, it feels like everyone has already made up their minds. Meanwhile, the students who work with you often continue to be treated disrespectfully. You know how important acceptance is to their self-esteem and you feel you need to take some action.

a) Identify the listening challenges that permeate this situation. Who isn't listening?
b) Decide what you can do to facilitate understanding, help students become more accepting of differences, and encourage respectful behavior.
c) Role play one or more of the conversations or presentations you suggest.

LISTENING APPLICATION 4

The Legal Environment

Application 4, Table 4

Desired Listening Outcomes: Legal Contexts	
Hearing Component: Desired Outcomes	
H1 Focus Attention on the Right Things	X
H2 Don't Get Distracted	X
H3 Hear the Message Accurately	
H4 Engage in Appreciative Listening	
Understanding Component: Desired Outcomes	
U1 Meet the Challenge of Individual Differences	
U2 Learn about Everything You Can	X
U3 Zero In on Key Points	X
U4 Reduce Interruptions	
Remembering Component: Desired Outcomes	
R1 Recognize Individual Factors that Affect Memory	
R2 Remember Names and Other Short-Term Memory Information	X
R3 Improve Your Long-Term Memory	
R4 Reduce the Factors that Negatively Affect Memory	

(*Continued*)

(Cont).

Desired Listening Outcomes: Legal Contexts

Interpreting Component: Desired Outcomes

I1 Develop Cognitive Empathy by Recognizing Individual Differences

I2 Develop Your EQ and Social Sensitivity for Perceptive Empathy   X

I3 Demonstrate Behavioral Empathy

Evaluating Component: Desired Outcomes

E1 Analyze Speaker Credibility   X

E2 Determine the Ethical Dimensions of the Situation   X

E3 Analyze Evidence and Reasoning   X

E4 Identify Emotional Appeals   X

E5 Listen Objectively

Responding Component: Desired Outcomes

RS1 Provide Clear and Direct Feedback

RS2 Increase Behavioral Flexibility   X

RS3 Develop Assertive Skills   X

RS4 Create a Supportive Communication Climate

Listening Contexts

Interpersonal   X

Team   X

Public

Mediated   X

Listening in the Legal Environment

Law is an important and exciting profession. Often, people think that a lawyer's most pressing challenges have to do with passing law courses and taking the Bar exam. Not so. To stand out in any aspect of the legal profession, you can readily differentiate yourself through effective listening behavior. As you might guess, listening in legal situations can be complicated. On the one hand, you need to observe and assess the interests and motivations of those involved directly in the case; but then, you also need to apply your critical listening to understand the complexities of the situation and the details of the opposing view. Not only will you need to listen to your client, but you may be taking depositions, listening to the judge, or listening to testimony that affects your position and decisions. Clearly, law is a dynamic and complex web of data, opinions, assumptions, and emotions. Sorting out these and other factors requires a great deal of focused listening.

Listening Challenges in the Legal Environment

As a lawyer, you have to love problem-solving! You will quickly discover that some challenges are inherent in the legal system, but others are introduced— intentionally or unintentionally—by one or more of the parties involved in your specific case as each attempts to influence and gain advantage.

When money and people's futures are at stake, listening can readily deteriorate. More than likely you will find yourself with the responsibility of sorting through the facts to develop a realistic and accurate assessment of the situation. The effectiveness of your listening behavior will determine the degree of your success.

Key Listening Outcome

1) Listen to assess client's perspective.
2) Ask appropriate questions.
3) Analyze evidence and reasoning.

Contexts: Interpersonal, team, mediated.

Cases in the Legal Environment

Case 1. Court Surprise

You love the thrill of being in a courtroom, but you find it stressful as well. You've spent the last several days preparing your case but, when the big day arrives, thinking on your feet is key. The prosecutor is experienced and you know he takes his challenge seriously. You think your client has told you everything you need to know about his grand theft charge, but as you listen to the prosecution you become worried about not being able to make a compelling argument. You know the judge will be looking for you to refute any accusations with strong and relevant evidence.

A witness has just taken the stand and is being asked some questions you didn't anticipate. She says she saw your client running from the jewelry store in a manner that would suggest guilt; yet, your client told you that while he was in the store around the time of the robbery, he walked out casually, still thinking about whether to make a purchase.

1) What listening challenges do you face in this situation?
2) What listening skills are required to be successful in this legal process?
3) What types of information are important to obtain?

Case 2. Look Before You Leap

Your client has provided you with detailed information about his case and you feel as if it is airtight.

There's a great deal of evidence that you've sorted through and you can't imagine that it won't be sufficient to win a judgment. After all, his six-year-old daughter fell into the neighbor's empty pool when no one was home and seriously injured her arm and ankle. She will likely have to walk with a limp for some time, and clearly it will mean she will not be able to participate in the usual sports activities so important to children that age.

As you understand it, the little girl was walking her dog in her back yard when Fluffy pulled the leash out of her hand and ran into the neighbor's yard. Of course she followed at a run and, suddenly, realized that she had stumbled into an old swimming pool that was difficult to see because of the weeds and ground cover that had grown around it. Without warning, she fell six feet onto the concrete.

Your client is not a greedy person but believes that there should be some consequence for this negligence and the suffering it caused. At the moment, you are deposing the neighbor whose pool was left abandoned and unattended. You can feel the tension as you walk into the room and introduce yourself. You explain that you have a few questions as you prepare your case, as you want to make sure all of your information is accurate. The neighbor seems extremely concerned about the child's welfare and asks a number of questions about how she is doing. As your conversation progresses, you discover the following.

- The neighbor has a fence around the pool; the child wiggled through a hole to get into the back yard.
- There are four signs that say "Danger: Please keep out"—one located on each side of the fence.
- When she was younger the child had gone swimming in the pool with her friends a number of times.
- There were also two "No trespassing" signs on the property as it is in the process of being sold and no one is currently living in the house.

1) What are your listening challenges?
2) What specific challenges do you confront when talking with each of the two parties?
3) What listening skills are most essential to reach a fair and reasonable outcome?
4) If you were to empathize with one of the individuals involved in the case, who would it be?

Case 3. Dazed and Confused

Sasha was still in a daze after her husband's massive heart attack. With a big family and quite a few assets, he told her that he wouldn't have peace of mind until she set up a trust. You generally have no problem in this type of fairly straightforward situation, and begin by asking her a number of basic questions about her properties and accounts. While you've been working as an attorney for several years, you can never recall dealing with someone who finds it so difficult to answer questions or stay on track. Whatever information you request somehow reminds her of something else and she begins talking about related but random details.

> I was thinking that Peter should be the executor; I know he took a law course once. But he's just so unreliable. Just last week he said he would call me to discuss this meeting but, guess what—right, never heard from him. Then there's Mia, but she is tied to her work, absolutely tied down by that awful supervisor of hers and I really don't think she'd make the time to do the job. No one gives me any input or useful information. I have to find out everything myself. It's not easy for me.

After the first 15 minutes you are completely confused and aren't sure how to pull things together so that you can provide the help she needs.

1) What are your listening challenges?
2) What do you see as your most important goal?
3) How might you approach the situation to be as productive as possible?
4) What specific listening skills will be particularly relevant?

Case 4. Power Play

You find your job as legal counsel for a large newspaper interesting and challenging. Your last appointment of the day is with one of the junior reporters, Ari. When he arrives you offer him coffee but he seems anxious and distracted, so you get right to business by asking what you can do for him. He explains that he has been trying hard to resolve the issue himself, but that he is being harassed by the news division chief, Martha Waltman. She has been relentless in making advances, which, until recently, he has been successful in blocking. Two nights ago she insisted that he drop off a hard copy of a major story he had been working on for nearly a month so that she could give him some feedback and advice before it went to press. When he stopped by her house to drop off the material, the situation became extremely awkward and she threatened to discredit one of his major sources if he didn't come in for an "intimate evening." He refused, telling her once again that he was in a relationship and that her advances were inappropriate and upsetting.

"I didn't want this situation to escalate," Ari says, shaking his head. "I tried to be clear and professional. But look," he holds out the morning's paper. "She took the entire article and gave herself credit—my name doesn't appear anywhere. Can you do something?"

You know immediately that there are steps you can take to explore the situation but you also realize how much influence Martha has over the entire operation and that any accusations are likely to result in a major blow-up for everyone.

1. What are the listening challenges in this situation?
2. What listening skills will you need to follow up on Ari's story?
3. What are your temptations—where might ethical issues arise?
4. How does credibility play a role in this situation?

The Legal Environment: If You Were There

Scenario 1. Got Credibility?

You are preparing for the second day of a case that has gone to trial. You were initially excited that you would have the opportunity to represent a woman you felt had been unfairly treated. She is an underrepresented minority and has worked hard all of her life; she was in the wrong place at the wrong time, and is accused of grand larceny. While you feel you did a thorough job presenting the facts of the case, for some reason you just weren't connecting with the jury yesterday. You tried to observe their reactions, but for the most part they seemed unmoved by your presentation. In fact, when they were dismissed, you overheard someone say that they felt sorry for the woman because she had such a junior, inexperienced lawyer defending her. You decide to take immediate action and ask a well-known coach and friend of the family for advice regarding how you might capture the jury's attention and gain the credibility you so desperately need in order to be successful.

a. You are the coach. What recommendations would you suggest to help this junior attorney gain credibility and convince the jury to take her seriously?
b. What might you do to gain credibility with the jury and maintain their attention?
c. Role play both scenarios for a minute or two. First, give a presentation that lacks conviction and poise. Then, deliver a case where credibility and confidence are clearly demonstrated. What variables affect listeners' perceptions?

Scenario 2. Toilet Troubles

You've just been hired to represent three college students who rent from Mr. Radcliffe. Radcliffe owns five rental properties in your small town, mainly occupied by students at the nearby university. You meet with the students to hear their complaints, which are substantial. All three attest to the fact that the unit is in very poor condition. They say they have complained on several occasions, especially about the toilet and sink faucet, which both leak constantly. The students explain that every time they bring up a problem, Mr. Radcliffe refuses to take it seriously and doesn't listen. He just shakes his head and says, "young people today—never understand them!" After nearly two months without resolution, the students agreed it was time to contact you. As you develop your response, you decide to talk with Mr. Radcliffe.

Your meeting with Mr. Radcliffe takes an unexpected turn when he shakes his head and laughs, pushing a signed contract toward you. Apparently there was full disclosure when the students agreed to rent from him, under an arrangement whereby they would make repairs to the apartment in exchange for reduced rent. From Mr. Radcliffe's perspective, he doesn't owe them anything. The students say they have no idea how to repair the problems they've encountered, and that Mr. Radcliffe is crazy and unreasonable to think they can "fix this junk." Mr. Radcliffe counters by emphasizing that the students knew exactly what they were agreeing to and that the conditions they complain about are their responsibility.

a. What listening issues can you identify?
b. What would be your next steps?
c. Role play a meeting with Mr. Radcliffe and the students in which you try to help them come to a mutual understanding.

LISTENING APPLICATION 5

Management and Leadership

Applications 5, Table 5

Desired Listening Outcomes: Manager and Leader	
Hearing Component: Desired Outcomes	
H1 Focus Attention on the Right Things	X
H2 Don't Get Distracted	
H3 Hear the Message Accurately	
H4 Engage in Appreciative Listening	
Understanding Component: Desired Outcomes	
U1 Meet the Challenge of Individual Differences	
U2 Learn about Everything You Can	X
U3 Zero In on Key Points	
U4 Reduce Interruptions	
Remembering Component: Desired Outcomes	
R1 Recognize Individual Factors that Affect Memory	
R2 Remember Names and Other Short-Term Memory Information	
R3 Improve Your Long-Term Memory	
R4 Reduce the Factors that Negatively Affect Memory	X

(Continued)

(Cont).

Desired Listening Outcomes: Manager and Leader

Interpreting Component: Desired Outcomes

I1 Develop Cognitive Empathy by Recognizing Individual Differences	X
I2 Develop Your EQ and Social Sensitivity for Perceptive Empathy	X
I3 Demonstrate Behavioral Empathy	

Evaluating Component: Desired Outcomes

E1 Analyze Speaker Credibility	
E2 Determine the Ethical Dimensions of the Situation	X
E3 Analyze Evidence and Reasoning	X
E4 Identify Emotional Appeals	
E5 Listen Objectively	X

Responding Component: Desired Outcomes

RS1 Provide Clear and Direct Feedback	X
RS2 Increase Behavioral Flexibility	
RS3 Develop Assertive Skills	X
RS4 Create a Supportive Communication Climate	X

Listening Contexts

Interpersonal	X
Team	X
Public	X
Mediated	X

Listening as Managers and Leaders

You may have heard leaders and managers described as "transformational," "autocratic," or "laissez-faire." While each theory has enjoyed popularity at one time or another, today's leader is largely distinguished by her ability and willingness to listen. As our vision for organizational effectiveness includes not only employee development but also employee empowerment, and as leaders recognize the importance of communicating values as well as goals, listening becomes one of the most essential skills. Leaders who focus on supporting their employees, who work to understand individual differences, and who are distinguished by their responsive and supportive style are called "servant leaders." These men and women are changing the nature of work as they create strong and sustaining listening environments where all employees feel free to express their ideas and realize their potential. A servant leader's emphasis on ethical leadership, and their concern for the development and welfare of all employees, further distinguishes their style.

Managers' and Leaders' Listening Challenges

The servant leadership philosophy assumes that most employees care about their work and want to do the best job possible. Servant leaders not only select and develop their employees, they motivate them toward a common, shared vision and empower them to participate fully in realizing these goals. There are, however, always unanticipated circumstances when challenges arise. Servant leaders have to have behavioral flexibility and assess whether their employees need additional coaching or training to act in the best interests of the organization. Listening in diverse organizational environments presents one of the most challenging, but important, leadership responsibilities as individual differences create both added value and complexity.

Key Listening Outcomes

1) Maintain high ethical awareness.
2) Listen to empower and support.
3) Demonstrate behavioral flexibility.

Context: Interpersonal, team, public, mediated.

Cases in Management and Leadership

Case 1. Two for One

One of your department heads, Mario, just retired. Two of his coworkers, Remi and June, each thought that they deserved his executive assistant and were sure that you would assign her to them. Remi argued that he was relatively new and had the largest region. Mario's former assistant, Jolene, would bring the experience he needed to support his efforts. June was livid when she realized that Remi was trying to get Jolene assigned to him. She had put in a request for Jolene months ago when she first heard of Mario's retirement. In addition, Remi was often impossible to understand and many of his coworkers felt he was impatient and difficult to work with. As a woman with seniority, she knew that Jolene would be much happier and more effective working with her.

You have scheduled a meeting with Remi and June to address this situation.

1) What listening challenges do you predict will arise at your meeting?
2) Considering Remi and June, what listening skills would make this situation more productive and most readily resolve the conflict?

3) How might you resolve this issue?
4) What specific listening skills will be most useful to you as you work to make this decision?
5) What you would say to Remi so that he knows you have listened to him?
6) What would you say to June so that she knows you have listened to her?

Case 2. Too Much of a Good Thing

You only have a few hours before a big report is due and you've been having computer issues all morning. Suddenly you realize that a member of your team, Sammy, is standing in your doorway watching you. She smiles and steps into your office as she begins to describe the new restaurant you had been thinking about trying out. Liam, who was delivering some of the materials you needed, overhears her description and joins in the conversation. "Did I hear you mention Bella Bella?" Liam asks as he sits on the edge of your desk. Just then Sammy's phone rings and she takes a short call from her daughter. When she is finished she begins again to describe Bella Bella's menu. She continues talking as the tech you called earlier regarding your computer issues finally arrives. After just a few minutes looking at your screen he begins to explain the steps you need to take to trouble shoot the issues you are having. He also provides a code and a phone number you can call if you need additional help. Sammy, who seems oblivious to his presence, continues talking about Bella Bella. Liam, when he isn't texting, continues asking Sammy questions and describing other places in town that she might try.

1) What listening challenges are going on with various parties in your office?
2) What listening challenges are you personally experiencing?
3) What actions might you take to improve the communication situation?
4) What listening skills will be most essential to accomplishing your goals?

Case 3. Gone with the Wind

You supervise a team of 20 well-trained sales personnel at a large furniture store. You have a good reputation and a long track record of satisfied customers. Recently, however, rumors have been circulating that the owners of your facility plan to downsize and reposition themselves in the market as a small custom retailer, perhaps even relocating to another town. Employees have gotten wind of change, and morale is at an all-time low. Your employees are distracted and fearful; they are having a difficult time focusing on customers and have begun arguing among themselves. Absenteeism has increased—you are concerned that your employees are out looking for new jobs. In addition, you know that misinformation is circulating and that the grapevine is running rampant.

You decide to hold a "town meeting" so that employees can ask you questions directly. You know how important it is to be forthcoming and transparent in times of change and you look forward to sharing what you know. Little did you anticipate, however, that the meeting would get out of control.

"I have a family of six," Sandy shouts. "I need to know whether or not I have a job!"

"Just because you have a big family doesn't make you so high and mighty," Perry responds. "I just took out a big loan. I've been a loyal employee for ten years. I deserve to be told what's going on!"

During the next 15 minutes, tensions increase and the insults and shouting escalate.

1) What are your listening challenges?
2) Develop an action plan—what should you do to recover and calm the fears? What goals are reasonable to expect in this situation?
3) What listening skills will be particularly important to apply?

Case 4. Telling It like It Is

You think that working in your family's small restaurant business will be a great life. Your two sisters, Sara and Jenny, are already employed and you look forward to joining them. Since you just graduated from business school you feel that you are even better prepared than your parents, who started the company over two decades ago, to run the show. They put a lot of confidence in you and within just a few months put you in charge of all of the company's human resources functions.

You are anxious to put into practice many of the systems and ideas you have learned, and soon you feel you have much better control on all phases of the process. You also spend a great deal of time on the floor, observing your staff and helping them to solve problems.

Because you try hard to be approachable, a number of your employees take advantage of your open-door policy and came in to talk with you. It seems that your older sister has been taking more than her share of the tips for quite some time. In addition, her coworkers describe situations where she has been eating meals and taking home food and occasionally even dishware. Since she is a member of the family, they hesitate to say anything to your parents—especially since it seems she is given other privileges, like holidays.

You know you need to address the situation, so you make an appointment with Sara to talk. She flatly denies taking additional tips, saying only that she works much harder than anyone else and, if her tips are higher, it's because she earned them. When confronted with eating unauthorized meals, she just laughs at you and says, "Hey little brother, you're the one with the big appetite! Just wait, you'll be ordering up huge plates of that pasta and seafood! So, bad me. Can I go now?"

1. What listening challenges do you anticipate?
2. What skills do you need to address this situation?
3. What skills do you need to determine the best course of action?
4. If things don't go well, what is likely to happen?

Management and Leadership: If You Were There

Scenario 1. Beef It Up

You're the manager of *Beef It Up*, a high-end restaurant in a large metropolitan area. You pride yourself on the quality of your food, particularly your beef. In fact, you advertise explicitly that you always use the highest-quality meats available in all your dishes. Unfortunately, your restaurant is going through some financial difficulties and the chef has proposed cutting the quality of meat in the stews and other preparations where, he has assured you and the owner, it won't be noticed. The restaurant owner is understandably concerned about finances, but has strong reservations about false advertising. In fact, he called the chef a "lying, knife-wielding manic" in their most recent emotional exchange on the issue. You are meeting that afternoon with the chef and the owner to make a decision about what to do. Both men have strong beliefs and become emotional and defensive very quickly. You feel your job is to get them to listen to each other and to come to an ethical and informed solution. You're not sure where to begin.

a. What do you see as the best outcome to the situation that could be achieved?
b. What specific approach should you take? How might you go about facilitating a productive conversation?
c. Role play the discussion you have with the chef and the owner.

Scenario 2. No Worries

You own a lawn care service in southwest Florida. Most of your business comes from wealthy neighborhoods so standards of care are high and you are very careful to hire only the most talented workers. Since your labor pool includes many non-native speakers of English, you have developed a number of communication strategies to make sure you understand what your workforce requires. Yesterday, however, you ran into a problem with one of your new customers, Dolly. Dolly just moved to Florida and wanted to make sure everything was done exactly right since she wasn't familiar with the Florida landscape. She spoke with two of your best employees and asked them to take care of a number of very specific tasks in preparation for a party she was holding. Apparently they nodded and assured her everything would be to her specifications. You just heard about the situation when Dolly called you, totally frustrated and angry. She explained that she had talked with your employees not once, but several times, and they apparently paid no attention to her. They nodded and promised to take care of things, but the jobs didn't get done. You realize that the problem was that they didn't understand her requests. You encourage all your clients to go through you to make their individual arrangements because your employees know little English and are embarrassed to admit this to the home owner. You realize that they nodded even though they had no idea what Dolly was asking them to do.

a. What are the listening challenges in this situation?
b. You are a manager with a very angry customer—what do you do?
c. What can you do to prevent this type of situation from recurring?

LISTENING APPLICATION 6

The Service Industry

Applications 6, Table 6

Desired Listening Outcomes: Service Industry

Hearing Component: Desired Outcomes

H1 Focus Attention on the Right Things	
H2 Don't Get Distracted	
H3 Hear the Message Accurately	X
H4 Engage in Appreciative Listening	

Understanding Component: Desired Outcomes

U1 Meet the Challenge of Individual Differences	X
U2 Learn about Everything You Can	X
U3 Zero In on Key Points	
U4 Reduce Interruptions	

Remembering Component: Desired Outcomes

R1 Recognize Individual Factors that Affect Memory	
R2 Remember Names and Other Short-Term Memory Information	X
R3 Improve Your Long-Term Memory	
R4 Reduce the Factors that Negatively Affect Memory	X

(Continued)

(Cont).

Desired Listening Outcomes: Service Industry

Interpreting Component: Desired Outcomes

I1 Develop Cognitive Empathy by Recognizing Individual Differences **X**

I2 Develop Your EQ and Social Sensitivity for Perceptive Empathy **X**

I3 Demonstrate Behavioral Empathy **X**

Evaluating Component: Desired Outcomes

E1 Analyze Speaker Credibility

E2 Determine the Ethical Dimensions of the Situation **X**

E3 Analyze Evidence and Reasoning

E4 Identify Emotional Appeals

E5 Listen Objectively **X**

Responding Component: Desired Outcomes

RS1 Provide Clear and Direct Feedback **X**

RS2 Increase Behavioral Flexibility **X**

RS3 Develop Assertive Skills

RS4 Create a Supportive Communication Climate

Listening Contexts

Interpersonal **X**

Team **X**

Public

Mediated **X**

Listening in the Service Industry

The service industry is growing and competition is increasingly based on the quality of the service encounter. Regardless of whether you work in a restaurant, hotel, bank, or in some form of tourism, effective listening is key to your ability to provide an outstanding and memorable service experience. While most of your interactions will be face-to-face, you may also find yourself interacting with customers on the phone or online. Regardless of the context, customers are seeking personalized, responsive service—they are seeking service employees who listen. If your goal is to distinguish yourself as an outstanding service employee or manager, your first step is to pay close attention to your customer or guest. Only when you get to know your customer can you determine her needs and work to satisfy them. This focus also makes your guest feel special and cared for, emotions that are associated with increased satisfaction and loyalty.

Listening Challenges in the Service Industry

Listening in the service sector isn't always easy. Customer expectations are often high, and the ease of getting information from the internet creates a situation where potential customers believe they already know a lot about your product. Misperceptions complicate your job of insuring satisfaction. In addition, customers themselves are often difficult and demanding, and expect a great deal of personalized attention. Your interactions with these individuals become part of the service experience and influence their perceptions and subsequent satisfaction. The good thing is that you're in a position to make a difference, to provide outstanding service through your customer focus—but only if you listen so that you accurately understand your customer's needs and priorities.

Key Listening Outcomes

1) Understand the customer's expectations and needs.
2) Accurately interpret the customer's nonverbal communication.
3) Respond appropriately to maintain the service relationship.

Contexts: Interpersonal, team, mediated.

Cases in the Service Industry

Case 1. Water Fights

You're the manager of a travel agency that increasingly does its business online. You work to keep your prices and inventory up-to-date and realize that you are serving the needs of a young, tech-savvy market. You are now on a live chat with one of your customers who feels she is particularly knowledgeable about the cruise industry. She just booked a cruise with you last week online and received several perks—a free drink package, free internet access, and $50.00 to spend on-board. She had booked an aft balcony stateroom and, in her subsequent surfing, she found the same stateroom for $200.00 less. She feels it is only fair that you match that price. Unfortunately, not only is it beyond the cancellation period, but you try to explain that the protection your agency provides and the free perks more than compensate for the difference in price. Realizing you are resisting her request, she immediately becomes more demanding and unreasonable.

1) What are the challenges of "listening" online?
2) How can you let this customer know you are listening to her?
3) How would you address this situation?
4) What listening skills will be particularly important?
5) What outcome or resolution would you be seeking?

Case 2. Business as Usual

You're excited to be working at the front desk of a business hotel in a large northeastern city. Your previous experience has been confined to local, small properties where there was little training and no career opportunities. You thought you were prepared for the convention rush of check-ins, but as your line gets longer you become increasingly stressed and disoriented. As you work as quickly as you can to accommodate arrivals, a young woman approaches the counter and, without hesitation, begins to explain the problems she's having with the business center. "I thought this was a business hotel. I have to finish up a presentation and make copies—nothing is working. Now I'll be late. I can't be late. Do you hear me? This is a really important meeting and nothing is working. This is the worst experience I've ever had in a hotel!"

You turn to try calm her down when a gentleman in line yells, "Missy, I'm a Gold member and was told there would be no wait."

1) What key listening challenges can you identify?
2) How can you best respond to the young woman?
3) How do you handle the line of check-ins?
4) What specific listening skills will you need?

Case 3. Sweet Dreams

You work as the assistant manager for an up-scale department store that specializes in home goods. One of your best-selling products this year has been memory foam for both pillows and beds. You have many repeat customers and pride yourself on understanding and addressing their needs. One of your loyal customers, Nida Gomez, approaches you.

> You know that memory foam you talked me into buying a couple of weeks ago? Well, it stinks. Literally. I had your people come over to take a look at it but all they said was 'Just wait.' I waited. Nothing happened. They brought over another mattress yesterday and it still stinks—I can't sleep in my own house, my whole bedroom smells. I had to take my family to a hotel last night because the 'new' mattress was so bad—and you're going to pay for it. I have a list here of what you owe me for all the inconvenience, and I want my money back for the mattress. And the hotel. And dinner.

Nida reaches in her pocket and hands you several receipts.

1) What listening challenges are described?
2) What further listening challenges do you anticipate?

3) How would you resolve this situation—and what factors influence your choices?
4) What listening skills will be particularly important to achieving your goal?
5) What would you consider an acceptable resolution?

Case 4. Best-Made Plans

You are the owner of a residential home-building company that prides itself on custom design. Your clients are generally wealthy couples looking to move up from their first or second homes. You are currently in the design process with a particularly well-respected couple who have been waiting for their children to leave so that they can build their dream home. In preparation for your fourth— and hopefully final—meeting with them, you have drafted the current plan and created a list of the decisions that have been made at previous sessions.

When the Bucknells arrive, you share your most recent floor plans and the list of requirements. Mrs. Bucknell studies the list, looks at the plan, and throws up her hands.

> This isn't what we decided! Ralph, you know I said I wanted a fireplace in the bedroom. Why doesn't it show? And the closet is way too small. Way too small. What happened?? I said, very clearly, that these were priorities. You may have expressed reservations at our last meeting but I certainly made my wishes clear!

Ralph shakes his head. "We did tell him to stick to our budget. Who needs a fireplace in the bedroom?"

Both parties look up at you, upset and frustrated.

1) What listening challenges can you identify?
2) What could have caused these misunderstandings?
3) What do you see as your role in this process?
4) What listening skills will you need to reduce tensions and move forward in a productive manner?

The Service Industry: If You Were There

Scenario 1. Cover for Me

You're the assistant manager at a quick service restaurant. While you love the challenges of management and believe your employees do a great job, you feel like you're in the middle of a no-win situation. Employees have been complaining loudly and regularly about working conditions, especially policies regarding staffing and covering shifts in emergency situations. Many of your employees are single parents and issues arise where they need to leave early or reschedule their shifts. Your manager refuses to even address the issue, and his lack of responsiveness to their concerns is hurting morale. He ignores their complaints and expresses no empathy for their personal needs. Consequently, employees complain about him in front of customers and have no incentive to do their best job.

a.   What should you do to create a stronger listening environment?
b.   Role play the scenario where you address this situation with employees and/or with your manager.

Scenario 2. No Limits

You work in convention services at a resort hotel where you are the wedding planner. Your job is to help the bride-to-be plan her dream wedding. In the past you have imported swans, hired bands from foreign countries, and had members of the wedding party flown in on your resort's private plane. Your motto is, "The sky isn't the limit—there is no limit!" While you love working with brides, it's generally the mothers that require all of your patience and tact. Your latest challenge is how to keep Mrs. Betty Shulman from ruining her daughter's day with too much of a good thing. Mrs. Shulman has requested sky divers jumping into the center of the dance floor, two giraffes flanking the altar area, and other "original" touches you feel are sure to end up causing confusion and chaos. While you don't believe the daughter really embraces her mother's requests, she doesn't speak up, so you're unsure what she thinks. On the other hand, you feel an obligation to express your reservations about many of the decisions that are being made. This candid response has not only created friction between you and Mrs. Shulman, it also hasn't resulted in any changes to her plans. You have no doubt that she is not really listening to a thing you say—should you just let it go?

a.   Why do you think the bride-to-be has remained silent? What does that communicate?
b.   What should you do next to achieve the most positive outcome possible in regard to both the wedding and the several relationships?
c.   Role play a conversation with both the mother and bride-to-be in which you work to facilitate effective listening among the three of you.

Recommended Reading for Part III

Ala-Kortesmaa, S. & Isotalus, P. (2015). Professional listening competence promoting well-being at work in the legal context. *International Journal of Listening*, 29, 30–49.

Asebedo, S. (2018). Planning for conflict in client relationships. *Journal of Financial Planning*, 1(10), 48–56.

Bennett, M. W. (2014). Eight traits of great trial lawyers. *The Review of Litigation*, 33(1), 1–44.

Berry, L. L. & Awdish, R. L. A. (2017, October 9). Making time to really listen to your patients. *Harvard Business Review*. https://hbr.org/2017/10/making-time-to-really-listen-to-your-patients.

Brownell, J. (2010). Leadership in the service of hospitality. *Cornell Hospitality Quarterly*, 51(3), 363–378.

Brownell, J. (2010). Listening leaders: The skills of listening-centered communication. *Listening and Human Communication in the 21st Century*, pp. 141–157. A. Wolvin (ed.). West Sussex: Blackwell Publishers.

Buelow, J. R. Mahan, P. L., & Garrity, A. W. (2010). Ethical dilemmas as perceived by healthcare students with teaching implications. *Journal of College Teaching and Learning*, 7(2), 85–92.

Chandra, S., Mohammadnezhad, M., & Ward, P. (2018). Trust and communication in a doctor-patient relationship: A literature review. *Journal of Healthcare Communication*, 36(3), 44–61.

Daimler, M. (2016, May 25). Listening is an overlooked leadership tool. *Harvard Business Review*. https://hbr.org/2016/05/listening-is-an-overlooked-leadership-tool.

de Vries, G., Jehn, K. A., & Terwel, B. W. (2011). When employees talk and managers don't listen. *Journal of Business Ethics*, 99, 4–7.

Duff, S. (2017). Empathy in leadership. *Training Journal*, 2, 9–11.

Flynn, J., Valikoski, T. R., & Grau, J. (2008). Listening in business context: Reviewing the status of research. *International Journal of Listening*, 22, 141–151.

Gaur, S. S., Xu, Y., & Quazi, A. (2011). Relational impact of service providers' interaction behavior in healthcare. *Managing Service Quality*, 21(1), 67–87.

Glynn, W. J., de Burca, S., & Brannick, T. (2003). Listening practices and performance in service organizations. *International Journal of Service Industry Management*, 14(3/4), 310–330.

Goby, V. P. & Lewis, J. H. (2000). The key role of listening in business: A study of the Singapore insurance industry. *Business Communication Quarterly*, 63, 41–50.

Hall, S. (2010). *Journey to Excellence in Hospitality Management: With Application for Service Industries in General*. Indianapolis, IN: Dog Ear Publishing.

Hewison, A., Sawbridge, Y., & Cragg, R. (2018). Leading with compassion in healthcare organizations. *Journal of Health Organization and Management*, 2(2), 338–354.

Hougaard, R. & Carter, J. (2018). Creating people-centric leadership and organizations. *Leadership Excellence*, 35(5), 40–42.

Jain, S. H. (2014, April 4). What it really takes to listen to patients. *Harvard Business Review*. https://hbr.org/2014/04/what-it-really-takes-to-listen-to-patients.

Johnston, M. K. & Reed, K. (2014). Listening environment and the bottom line: How a positive environment can improve financial outcomes. *International Journal of Listening*, 31, 71–79.

Kharbanda, O. P. & Stallworthy, E. A. (2001). Listening—A vital negotiating skill. *Journal of Managerial Psychology*, 6(4), 6–8.

MacLeod, L. (2016). Listening: More than what meets the ear. *Physician Leadership Journal*, 3(4), 14–19.

McClellan, J. & DiClementi, G. (2017). Emotional intelligence and positive organizational leadership: A conceptual model for positive emotional influence. *Journal of Behavioral and Applied Management*, 17(3), 197–212.

Mercieca, C., Cassar, S., & Borg, A. A. (2014). Listening to patients: Improving the outpatient service. *International Journal of Health Care Quality Assurance*, 27(1), 44–53.

Pedersen, A. R. (2016). The role of patient narratives in healthcare. *Journal of Health Organization and Management*, 30(2), 244–257.

Rennaker, M. A. (2008). *Listening and Persuasion: Examining the Communicative Patterns of Servant Leadership*. Dissertation, Regent University, Virginia Beach, VA. AAT 3309285.

Roberts, J. V. (2009). Listening to the crime victim: Evaluating victim input at sentencing and parole. *Crime and Justice*, 8(1), 56–71.

Sadri, G. (2015). Empathy in the workplace. *Industrial Management*, 57(5), 22–27.

Scanlan, L. (2011). Listening: Executive skill most wanting? *Healthcare Financial Management*, 65(10), 116–118.

Singh, P. & Gandhi, N. (2017, November 6). Listening is a lost art in medicine. Here's how to rediscover it. *Harvard Business Review*. Accessed January 22, 2019. https://hbr.org/2017/11/listening-is-a-lost-art-in-medicine-heres-how-to-rediscover-it.

Worthington, J. (2018). Taking the doctor-patient relationship to another level: Patients. *The Australian Financial Review*, 2, 46–47.

Xu, Y., Yap, S., & Hyde, K. (2016). Who is talking, who is listening? Service recovery through online customer-to-customer interactions. *Marketing Intelligence & Planning*, 34(3), 421–444.

INDEX